Caring for an overweight cat

by Andrea Harvey and Samantha Taylor

Published by Vet Professionals

Copyright © Vet Professionals 2012

www.vetprofessionals.com

ISBN 978-1-908583-00-0

About Cat Professional

Cat Professional is a subdivision of Vet Professionals Ltd. Cat Professional was founded in 2007 by Dr Sarah Caney with the aims of providing cat owners and veterinary professionals with the highest quality information, advice, training and consultancy services.

catprofessional.com

Publications

Cat Professional is a leading provider of high quality publications on caring for cats with a variety of medical conditions. Written by international experts in their field, each book is written to be understood by cat owners and veterinary professionals. The books are available to buy through the website www.catprofessional.com as eBooks where they can be downloaded and read instantly. Alternatively they can be purchased as a softback via the website and good bookstores.

'Caring for an overweight cat' was first published in January 2012. Other books in the Cat Professional series include:

- 'Caring for a cat with chronic kidney disease' by Dr Sarah Caney

- 'Caring for a blind cat' by Natasha Mitchell

- 'Caring for a cat with hyperthyroidism' by Dr Sarah Caney

- 'Caring for a cat with lower urinary tract disease' by Dr Sarah Caney and Professor Danièlle Gunn-Moore

A variety of free-to-download articles also feature on the Cat Professional website.

Advice, Training and Consultancy

Cat Professional is dedicated to improving the standards of cat care and in this capacity is a provider of Continuing Professional Development to veterinary surgeons, veterinary nurses and other professionals working with cats around the world.

Cat Professional also works closely with leading providers of cat products and foods providing training programmes, assisting with product literature and advising on product design and marketing.

Specialist feline medicine advice is available to veterinary professionals and cat owners world-wide. Details are available on the website.

About the authors

Andrea Harvey graduated from the University of Bristol Veterinary School in 2000. Andrea spent a year and a half in various small animal practices, and during this time realised that she wanted to focus her career on working with cats and their owners. She was therefore thrilled to be appointed as the Feline Advisory Bureau (FAB) Scholar back at Bristol Vet School in 2002, to begin training as a feline specialist. Andrea gained the RCVS Diploma in Feline Medicine and the European Diploma in Veterinary Internal Medicine in 2005 and became a Royal College of Veterinary Surgeons (RCVS) Recognised Specialist in Feline Medicine in 2006. She stayed on at Bristol Vet School as FAB lecturer from 2005-2010, and currently works freelance as a feline specialist, working in various clinics and working closely with the FAB and International Society of Feline Medicine. Andrea is passionate about all aspects of cat care, and has written many articles and lectures on feline medicine all over the world. Andrea currently lives in Somerset with two very handsome cats, Jack and Thomas.

Samantha Taylor graduated from the Royal Veterinary College in 2002, fulfilling her lifelong ambition to be a vet. She initially worked in a large referral (second opinion) practice and then in a small animal practice in Cambridge where her interest in cats really started, and she enjoyed running feline only clinics. She returned to referral practice in 2005 and studied for the Royal College of Veterinary Surgeons Certificate in Internal Medicine which she passed in 2006. That year she started a Feline Advisory Bureau residency at Bristol University and loved working with cats and their owners. She obtained the European Diploma in Veterinary Internal Medicine in 2009 and in 2011 became an RCVS Recognised Specialist in Feline Medicine. She has published scientific papers and written many articles on various feline medicine subjects. She currently lives in Wiltshire with her husband, little boy (Alex) and two mischievous cats.

About this book

This book has been written as both a printed book and an interactive electronic book.

Words in blue are contained in the glossary section at the end of the book.

Acknowledgements

The authors would like to thank the owners of the cats featured in this book for allowing them to include their stories, and all the cats that graciously posed for photographs! Thanks also go to colleagues and friends for their contributions and advice during the writing of the book, particularly Richard Malik, Susan Little, Vicky Halls, Nicola Ackerman, Nikki Gaut and Rebecca Giles.

We also thank the Feline Advisory Bureau who have funded both Andrea and Samantha's positions throughout their specialist training, enabling them to become feline Specialists.

The authors would like to acknowledge the following people for providing images for this book; Martin Owen, Anne Fawcett, Erin Bell, Vicky Halls, Tim Knott, The Oxford Cat Clinic, The University of Bristol, Kitten to Cat Clinic and The Feline Advisory Bureau.

Thanks go to Sarah Caney for the concept of this book and useful input at the editing stage, as well as her continuing inspiration and support as a colleague and friend.

The authors would like to dedicate this book to a couple of cats who have made a big impact on their lives. Bruno, a rather overweight cat himself who spent his retirement with Samantha after years of helping other cats as a blood donor, and George, an elderly overweight cat that Andrea rescued from euthanasia in her first job and was a loving companion during all her specialist training, as well as teaching her all the tricks for achieving weight loss in cats!

CONTENTS

A cat is described as overweight if it is 10% or more heavier than its ideal body weight. We often read in the news that human obesity is on the increase, the resulting health problems are well known, and we are inundated with different diet trends and weight loss plans. Now this trend has spilled over into the feline community and veterinary professionals are increasingly presented with overweight cats. The modern pet cat lives a very different life to the rat-catching farm cat and as a result of this easier and more comfortable living, and different way of feeding, is more prone to gaining weight. To be told that your cat is overweight or even obese can be very upsetting news. As a loving carer we feel guilty that we have had some part to play in the problem. You may also be very worried about the health implications of your cat's weight and have concerns about putting them on a strict or tasteless diet. However, with good advice and support, overweight cats can lose weight in a healthy way, avoid many health problems and live a long and happy life. The aim of this book is to give care providers more information on obesity and weight gain in cats: the causes, resulting health problems, and importantly management and prevention. In addition to the recommendations made by your veterinary practice, this book will provide you with tips for improving health and wellbeing that are neither time-consuming nor involve starving your cat.

The modern pet cat lives a very different life to the rat-catching farm cat.

The difference between an overweight cat, and a fit healthy weight cat can be seen in these photographs.

Why is my cat overweight?

This may be the first question you want to ask if you are told that your cat is overweight. We all want the best for our pets and to feel that something we have done has adversely affected our cat's health can be very upsetting. The fact is that weight gain and obesity are the result of your cat taking in more calories (calories are units of energy in food and drink, which if consumed to excess will lead to weight gain) than they expend. Simply put, this means they are eating too much and moving around too little. In some cases these facts are not easily apparent, such as the cat that is eating elsewhere and multi-cat households where one cat may be stealing another's food. Occasionally weight gain can result from other health problems, but in the vast majority of cases weight gain is a direct result of overeating. Of course this is almost always unintentional, due to feeding the wrong type or

amount of food (containing excessive calories), and feeding it in the wrong way, in combination with a cat's inactive lifestyle.

One of the pleasures of owning a pet is to provide them with food they enjoy and to see our cat tucking enthusiastically into a plate of food, to us as carers indicates health and happiness. We enjoy our food so why shouldn't our cat? It is important to remember that eating is not a social event for cats, as it is for humans. If your cat is overweight, it is likely they have enjoyed their food a bit too much!

Is my cat going to be at risk of illness as a result of being overweight or obese?

Just as obese humans are more likely to suffer health problems, so are overweight and obese cats. People tend to naturally perceive that thin and emaciated cats are unwell, but often perceive overweight cats to be healthy, whereas in fact being overweight can mean just as serious health concerns as being too thin. These problems may be present now, at the time your cat is noted to be overweight or they may develop in the future if your cat fails to lose weight. Many overweight and obese cats seem perfectly healthy and so it can be hard to make the efforts

> **We are all guilty of giving our cat another treat when they purr and an extra spoon of their favourite food.**

required to change things. However it is important to think ahead; overweight cats are storing problems for the future which may shorten their life span, result in chronic health problems (and large veterinary bills) and importantly reduce their quality of life. Therefore it is vital to tackle the problem as soon as it is identified and this way prevent your cat developing any of the conditions described in **Section 2** of this book. If your cat already has an obesity related illness then weight loss is imperative to improve your cat's health.

Could I have prevented this from happening – is it my fault?

When other unusual causes of weight gain have been excluded by your veterinarian, it is true that in most cases the obesity, as mentioned above, is caused by overeating and inactivity. Therefore when you are told your cat is overweight or obese the first emotions you are likely to feel are denial, or guilt. As the provider of food, in the majority of cases, we as carers control our cat's food intake. We choose what to buy from the pet shop or supermarket and we put this food into our cat's bowl. We also all lead very busy lives and as such when in a hurry maybe we do put a little too much in the bowl, or without thinking use feeding as a way of keeping our cats occupied when we are busy. However, there is no use in blaming yourself. As a loving care provider you will not have intended to cause your cat any harm, perhaps you have had other cats and fed them identically and had no problems, perhaps you even have more than one cat and the other cat eats the same food and is slim. What is important is discussing with your veterinarian how to change your cat's diet and activity levels to result in healthy, steady weight loss. We are all guilty of giving our cat another treat when they purr and an extra spoon of their favourite food, but now you can learn what treats are appropriate and how many spoons your cat should be eating, and when we need to draw the line.

I feel guilty because I don't have much time to interact with my cat

Modern life can be busy and stressful. You may have other pets, children, a busy job and many demands on your time. This doesn't mean you are not a loving care provider; we simply have to learn ways of feeding and playing with our cats that use our precious time in the best way. Even a short period of playing with your cat, if done regularly, ideally daily, and combined with an appropriate diet will make a difference. Most people do not have a huge amount of spare time therefore this book aims to teach time-efficient ways to manage your cat's weight. You will also discover lots of innovative ways of increasing your cat's activity that don't necessarily involve extra time and work for you!

I'm going to feel cruel restricting food intake

As mentioned previously, a joy of pet ownership is feeding. Therefore when considering a diet for your cat you may envisage a hungry and angry kitty begging for more food. Modern diets designed for weight management in cats have taken into account the need for your cat to enjoy their food and to feel full after eating it, so you may be surprised that they protest little

A weight loss diet doesn't necessarily mean your cat will be left hungry.

and still enjoy tucking in. Certainly if your cat is used to large volumes of food, or tasty (but high calorie) treats, then furry noses may be put a little out of joint. The old phrase 'being cruel to be kind' is often used here. However, starving a cat, or restricting their food significantly is not advised and a carefully planned, gradual weight loss programme, combined with increased exercise should certainly not be cruel, and your cat will soon adjust to the new routine. Different ways of feeding will also stimulate them and give them other things to think about, and help them enjoy their food lasting a longer period of time, instead of being tempted to just stand by the food bowl and overeat! Remember you are doing this for your cat's long term health and wellbeing and that fattening treats now can cause severe health problems later.

In this section of the book we will discuss why cats become overweight and what can be done to treat and prevent it.

What is obesity?

Obesity is excessive fat deposition, which can lead to a variety of health problems. Obesity is often defined as when a cat weighs around 15-20% more than they should, i.e. 15-20% heavier than their ideal body weight. For example, a cat with an ideal body weight of 4.4kg would be classed as obese once they weighed 5kg or more. It is difficult to define obesity precisely, but in general this condition means that your cat is significantly heavier than they should be and that their health is likely to suffer as a result. Obviously being just a little overweight is also a problem, as this small weight gain, year on year, will eventually result in obesity.

How do I know that my cat is overweight or obese?

It can be hard to decide if your cat is the correct weight, just a little overweight, or actually obese. Regular weighing is always important in helping to detect steady, even subtle, trends in weight change, before a large change in weight becomes obviously apparent. Small changes in weight can sometimes seem insignificant, but when put into context of the small size of a cat, a small change in weight can be proportionately very significant.

So, anytime your cat has changed weight, it is useful to calculate the percentage change in weight.

Percentage change in weight = (current weight — previous weight)/previous weight

Since with cats we are looking at small changes in weight, it is important that scales used are accurate at low weights (at least to the nearest 100 grams). It can be difficult to accurately weigh your cat at home; balancing on the bathroom scales is bound to

For example, Jack weighed 5.1kg at his annual vaccination last year. This year he weighs 5.5kg. 0.4kg weight gain seems like a tiny amount, but if we calculate his % change in weight: (5.5-5.1)/5.1 = 8% weight gain

This would be equivalent to a person weighing 65kg (143 pounds or 10 stones and 3 pounds), gaining around 5.2kg (11.5 pounds) in a year, which I think most people would agree is really quite a lot! Certainly well over one dress size!

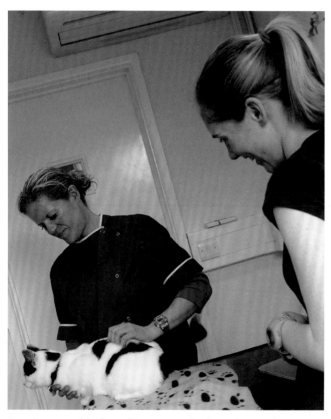

Assessing your cat's body condition score can be done at home, or by your veterinarian and is simple and easy.

be inaccurate! If you have accurate digital scales that allow placement of the cat's carrier on them, then weighing in the carrier is the best option. Using the same scales to minimise inaccuracies as a result of variation between scales is also important. Your veterinary practice will have specially designed scales to be accurate at low weights, and so these are the ideal ones to be used wherever possible. You can also purchase your own suitable scales designed for weighing babies. These are often reasonably priced and can be a worthwhile investment for use during a weight loss programme.

Although weighing regularly is important, just relying on the scales may be misleading, as the correct weight for your cat may not be the same as for another cat. This is certainly true amongst pure breeds; a large Maine Coon will of course weigh more than a petite Abyssinian. Therefore an alternative way to assess your cat's size is by measuring body condition score. This is simple, can be done at home and may provide an early indication that your cat is overweight. A cat's body weight at about one year of age is usually about what their ideal weight should be, since weight gain usually occurs after this. Therefore recording, and looking back to your cat's weight at one year of age is a useful guide.

Body condition score

There are several guides and scales available to demonstrate how to measure body condition and grade on either a five point or nine point scale, the higher number indicating more fat carried. The cat's body condition score is assessed by running your hands along the ribcage, looking at the cat from the side and from above and allocating a number on the scale. Different pet food companies may have different scales. The Purina system allocates a 9 to an obese cat and a 1 to a very underweight cat as shown in the chart (courtesy of Purina).

Body Condition Tool

PURINA

Too Thin

1 — Severely Underweight
- Ribs, backbone and hip bones all highly visible[1] with complete absence of any fat
- Severely exaggerated waistline[2]
- Tummy non-existent[3]

2 — Very Thin
- Ribs and backbone easily seen[1] with no overlying fat layer
- Exaggerated waistline[2]
- Severe tummy tuck[3]

3 — Thin
- Ribs and backbone are easily felt and seen[1] with minimal overlying fat layer
- Noticeable waistline[2]
- Distinct tummy tuck with no belly fat[3]

4 — Slightly Underweight
- Ribs can be felt and may/may not be seen[1] with very thin layer of overlying fat
- Obvious waistline[2]
- Slight tummy tuck with minimal belly fat[3]

Ideal

5 — Ideal Weight
- Ribs can be felt and may/may not be seen[1] with a small layer of overlying fat
- A clear waistline can be seen[2]
- Visible tummy tuck[3]

Too Heavy

6 — Overweight
- Ribs can be felt but generally can't be seen[1] with a distinct layer of overlying fat
- Waistline is not clear[2]
- Tummy may bulge slightly outwards and sag downwards[3], with a small fat pad

7 — Very Overweight
- Ribs are hard to feel and see[1] with a thickened layer of overlying fat
- Waistline is difficult to see[2]
- Tummy bulges outwards and may sag downwards[3], with noticeable fat pad that may wobble when cat moves

8 — Obese
- Ribs can't be felt or seen with a very thick layer of overlying fat
- Additional fat pads present over the lower back
- Waistline is absent[2]
- Tummy bulges outwards and sags downwards[3], with obvious fat pad that probably wobbles or sways when cat moves

9 — Clinically Obese
- Ribs are impossible to feel with a marked layer of very thick overlying fat
- Additional heavy fat pads are noticeable over the lower back, legs and around the face
- Waistline is absent[2]
- Tummy distinctly bulges outwards and sags downwards[3], with a substantial fat pad that wobbles or sways when cat moves

[1] In short-haired cats. [2] When viewed from above. [3] When viewed from the side. The Body Condition System was developed at the Nestlé Purina Petcare Centre and has been validated in the following publications: Laflamme DP. Feline Practice 1997; 25:13-17. Laflamme et al. Compendium 2001; 23 (Suppl 9A):88

A 5 point scale may also be used (image courtesy of Royal Canin).

Body Condition Score – Feline

Body Condition Score	Characteristics
1 **Very Thin** More than 20% below ideal body weight	■ Ribs, spine and pelvic bones are easily visible (in short haired pets) ■ Obvious loss of muscle mass ■ No palpable fat on chest
2 **Thin** Between 10 and 20% below ideal weight	■ Ribs, spine and pelvic bones visible ■ Obvious waist ■ Minimal abdominal fat
3 **Ideal Weight**	■ Ribs, spine and pelvic bones not visible but easily palpable ■ Obvious waist ■ Little abdominal fat
4 **Overweight** 20% above ideal weight	■ Ribs, spine and pelvic bones are hardly palpable ■ Waist is absent ■ Heavy abdominal fat deposits
5 **Markedly Obese** 40% above ideal weight	■ Massive fat deposits on chest, spine and the abdomen ■ Obviously distended abdomen

The Body Condition Score combines the evaluation of visible characteristics and palpitation of certain areas of the body. The scoring system offers the advantage of being easy to use by the veterinary surgeon or veterinary nurse and also by the owner and can be applied both for diagnosis of obesity and active presentation. Nutritional recommendations may be made following body condition scoring which will vary in relation to the cat's lifestyle (indoors, outdoors), his age and level of activity.

An alternative guide is the S.H.A.P.E. (size, health and physical examination) by Waltham/Royal Canin which uses letters instead of numbers and a flow chart to allocate a condition score based on physical assessment and adding assessment of health or movement problems.

The WALTHAM® S.H.A.P.E.™ guide
The WALTHAM® S.H.A.P.E.™ guide uses a flowchart to classify pets into one of seven categories. This approach is specifically designed to be used by owners with no prior experience or training and has been successfully validated against clinical measures of body composition.

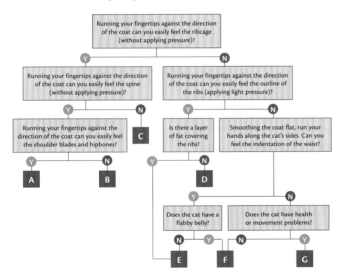

S.H.A.P.E.™ Score	Description
A	Extremely thin – your cat has a very small amount or no total body fat. Recommendation: seek veterinary advice promptly.
B	Thin – your cat has only a small amount of total body fat. Recommendation: seek veterinary advice to ensure your cat is being offered the appropriate amount of food. Reassess using the S.H.A.P.E.™ chart every 2 weeks.
C	Lean – your cat is at the low end of the ideal range with less than normal body fat. Recommendation: increase food offered by a small amount. Monitor monthly using the S.H.A.P.E.™ chart and seek veterinary advice if no change.
D	Ideal – your cat has an ideal amount of total body fat. Recommendation: monitor monthly to ensure your cat remains in this category and have him/her checked by the veterinarian at your next visit.
E	Mildly overweight – your cat is at the upper end of the ideal range with a small amount of excess body fat. Recommendation: seek veterinary advice to ensure your cat is being offered the appropriate amount of food and try to increase activity levels. Avoid excessive treats and monitor monthly using the S.H.A.P.E.™ chart.
F	Moderately overweight – your cat has an excess of total body fat. Recommendation: seek veterinary advice to implement safely an appropriate weight loss plan including increasing activity levels. Reassess using the S.H.A.P.E.™ chart every 2 weeks.
G	Severely overweight – your cat has a large amount of excess total body fat that is affecting its health and well being. Recommendation: seek veterinary advice promptly to introduce a weight loss plan to reduce your cat's weight. Increase activity levels and improve overall health.

NB: Some breeds and different life-states may have different ideal S.H.A.P.E.™ scores. Consult your veterinarian if you are unsure.

Waltham/Royal Canin have also developed an alternative way of assessing a cat's body condition called the 'Feline Body Mass Index'. This is calculated by measuring the ribcage circumference and the length of the lower leg (as shown in the pictures) and plotting onto a graph. Measurement of a 'body mass index' is also used in human medicine using height and weight.

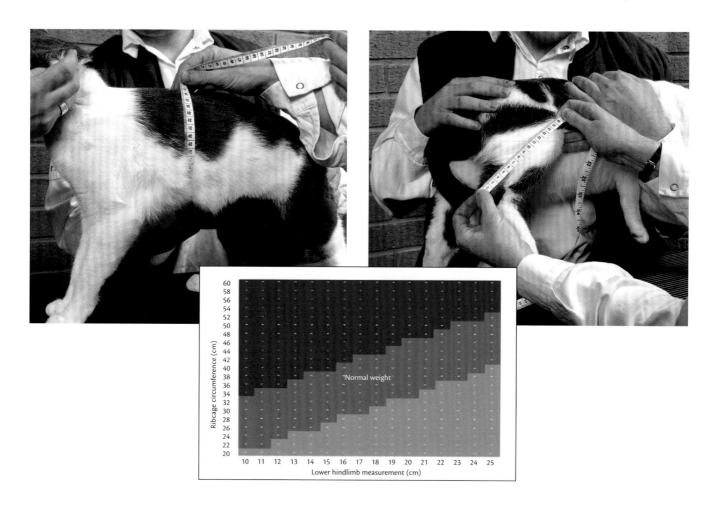

Why worry about my cat's weight?

Being overweight will have many effects on your cat's life and health. Some diseases are known to be caused or aggravated by excess body fat (see later in this chapter) but being overweight can also make daily life more challenging and uncomfortable.

What are the general consequences of being overweight?

■ Moving around

A healthy cat is a lithe and flexible creature, able to jump high fences easily. Being overweight can reduce this mobility and therefore result in the cat being less mobile and interacting less with other pets and family members. It may also mean that they are unable to use their cat flap and therefore are unable to get outside to exercise. This reduced movement then perpetuates the weight gain as the less they move, the fewer calories are burnt, not to mention a reduced quality of life.

■ Grooming

Cats are by nature fastidious about cleanliness. They spend several hours a day grooming their coat to remove dirt and tangles. This is important for their health, as well as being part of normal cat behaviour and well-being. Overweight cats can find it difficult to reach some parts of their body to groom them and therefore fail to remove faeces or urine from the coat resulting in skin irritation, infection and even in extreme cases maggot infestation. Lack of grooming can also mean a tangled or matted coat which can pull the skin and cause pain and damage the skin. Keeping clean by effectively grooming themselves is very important and being unable to do this can have a negative impact on a cat's quality of life.

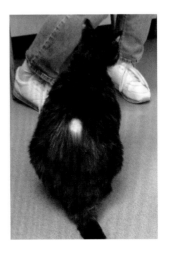

Overweight cats can find it difficult to groom themselves – the overweight cat in this picture cannot reach far enough to groom her rear, so has over-groomed her back leading to hair loss.

Anaesthesia poses greater risks in an overweight cat.

■ Risk of anaesthetic complications

If your cat needs to be anaesthetised at any stage, for example for repair of a wound, tooth removal, or more major surgery, simply being overweight will increase the risk associated with anaesthesia. Being overweight or obese can also increase the complexity, and therefore risk, of the surgery.

■ Reduced immune function (defence against infection)

In people, obesity is associated with reduced immune function, and this may be true in cats too, making them more susceptible to certain illnesses and infections.

■ Heat intolerance

Being overweight makes cats much more intolerant of the heat meaning they are very uncomfortable in warmer weather. This can be a particular issue in countries with warmer climates and during summer months.

■ Effect on breathing

As in people, being overweight means more effort is required for breathing, and overweight cats can easily become breathless if they over-exert themselves, for example if they need to run away from another animal.

■ Quality of life

A healthy cat should enjoy life, be keen to move around, play, and interact with the family. If being overweight stops your cat doing these things then they do have a reduced quality of life, something as a loving carer we hate to see. By helping your cat lose weight and get moving you are not only improving their physical condition, but also their enjoyment of life.

What illnesses are associated with being overweight?

■ Diabetes mellitus

Obesity is a common cause of diabetes in cats. This occurs because being overweight interferes with the action of the hormone insulin, resulting in elevated levels of sugar (glucose) in the blood (hyperglycaemia). Middle aged to older aged cats are at greatest risk of developing diabetes.

What to look for in your cat

Signs that carers may notice include an increase in thirst and urination, and an increase in appetite. However, early in the course of the disease you may not notice anything is wrong with

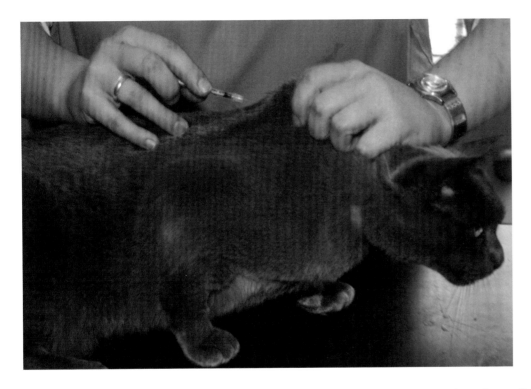

A cat being injected with insulin to treat diabetes mellitus.

your cat. Also, if your cat goes outside to urinate and drink, then some of these signs may be missed. If diabetes goes untreated for a prolonged period of time, more serious effects of the diabetes can occur, such as vomiting, loss of appetite, weakness and eventually collapse. This can even result in death in severe cases.

Diagnosis and treatment
Diabetes is diagnosed by demonstrating a persistent elevation in blood sugar (glucose) and involves doing blood and urine tests. Normally, treating diabetes means having to inject your cat with insulin on a daily basis (normally twice daily), for the rest of its life. Frequent trips to the veterinary practice are required throughout to constantly adjust the dose of insulin in order to stabilise the diabetes, and to monitor for complications that can arise as a result of the diabetes.

Routine health checks including urine checks can help pick diabetes up early. This is particularly important in overweight cats, because if the diabetes is picked up and treated promptly and weight is effectively managed, then there is a good chance that the diabetes may only be 'transient', for example resolving over a period of weeks or months. This means that it is possible that insulin injections are only required temporarily.

Of course, it is better not to risk permanent diabetes occurring at all, and preventing or managing weight gain before it has led to diabetes in the first place is clearly preferable.

■ **Osteoarthritis**

Osteoarthritis is a condition where the joints become inflamed and painful. It is a well recognised problem in humans and dogs, but only relatively recently recognised in cats. It is thought to be a common problem in older cats. However, cats are masters of concealing pain and show few signs meaning that this diagnosis can be overlooked.

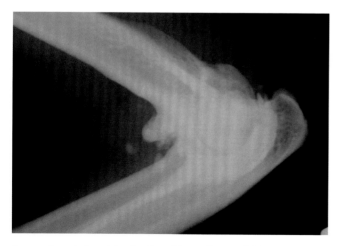

An xray of a cat's elbow joint showing evidence of osteoarthritis.

Cats with osteoarthritis rarely limp and instead show subtle signs of pain.

Although being overweight is not in itself a sole cause of osteoarthritis, it can contribute to its development, because when an athletic animal jumps and lands (often onto hard ground, taking most weight onto the forelimbs) all that extra weight puts abnormal pressure on the joints. This predisposes the joints to damage and increases the risk of developing osteoarthritis. Once the joints have become damaged, carrying excessive weight will certainly make sore joints even more uncomfortable. An affected cat will be understandably reluctant to move due to pain and therefore can gain even more weight from the resulting inactivity. Part of the management protocol for overweight cats will include increasing movement, but a cat with osteoarthritis will be reluctant to play or move around. Therefore it is important to identify and manage this condition along side the weight management.

What to look for in your cat

As cats are so good at hiding their pain it can be very difficult to know if your cat has osteoarthritis. They are not taken for walks and are often affected in more than one limb so limping is rarely noticed. Cats also rarely vocalise their pain, preferring to withdraw from family life and restrict their own movement. Signs you may notice include:

■ Reduced mobility
  – Reluctance to jump up or down from furniture

- Sleeping in different, easier to access (lower) sites
- Difficulty using the cat flap
- Lameness/limping – as mentioned this is less commonly noticed
- Stiff/stilted gait
- Litter tray accidents, missing the tray, reluctance to climb into high sided trays

■ Changes in grooming behaviour
  - Matted and scurfy coat (may also be related to weight gain)
  - Over-grooming painful joints

■ Temperament changes
  - Reduced interaction i.e. lack of response to petting
  - Lack of tolerance of handling, of children, and of other pets
  - Changes in activity level (which may also relate to weight gain)
  - Playing and going outside less frequently
  - Not hunting or exploring the outdoor environment as frequently
  - Overgrown claws due to lack of activity

Diagnosis and treatment

It is very important to consult your veterinarian if your cat shows any of the signs listed above. Diagnosis of osteoarthritis is often made on the basis of information gathered from a history and physical examination. Your veterinarian may also need to see your cat walking and, in some cases, x-rays are performed to confirm the diagnosis. Your veterinarian will be able to advise you on weight management and if appropriate they may prescribe painkillers to make your cat more comfortable. This will help to encourage your cat to move around more. Once your cat starts to lose weight you may notice that the signs of osteoarthritis improve and in some cases pain killers are no longer required.

■ **Lower urinary tract disease**

Diseases of the bladder are a frequent group of disorders encountered in cats. The most common type is a disease called 'Feline Idiopathic Cystitis', a form of sterile (i.e. not caused by bacterial infection) cystitis (inflammation of the bladder wall). There are many contributing factors involved in causing the condition, but being overweight is one risk factor.

What to look for in your cat

The disorder results in discomfort on urination, so carers may notice their cat paying frequent trips to the litter tray and excessively straining, and only passing small amounts of urine, bloody urine or none at all. The urethra (the tube from the bladder to outside) can become completely blocked, not allowing any passage of urine. This is of particular concern in male cats. If this happens the condition is serious, and can even lead to fatal complications. Other cases may be more mildly affected, but the condition often recurs and is extremely uncomfortable.

Diagnosis and treatment

Diagnosis involves your veterinarian taking a careful history from you about your cat's signs, examining your cat, analysing the urine, and may also involve excluding other diseases by doing an ultrasound examination and/or taking x-rays. There are many different aspects of treatment such as anti-inflammatories, pain relief and environmental enrichment to reduce stress. However, weight management, together with dietary change and increasing water intake are also important factors in managing the condition. Cystitis is discussed in much greater detail in the Cat Professional publication 'Caring for a cat with lower urinary tract disease'.

■ Constipation

Constipation is a very unpleasant and uncomfortable condition for your cat. Constipation is the medical term for reduced frequency or difficulty passing faeces. Affected cats may be uncomfortable and can be seen straining to pass firm, dry stools.

Overweight cats can become constipated. This litter tray has had one side removed to make it easier for an overweight cat (or a cat with osteoarthritis) to climb into.

Overweight cats are unfortunately prone to developing constipation for a variety of reasons including:

■ Reluctance to move – exercise and moving also 'moves' the digestive system. A sedentary life leads to a sluggish bowel

■ Difficulty using the litter tray – cats are very clean by nature and if the litter tray is difficult to get into (due to their size or concurrent osteoarthritis) then they will 'hold on' resulting in constipation

■ Not drinking enough – if an overweight cat is reluctant to move and therefore drinks less, they can become dehydrated causing faeces (stools) to become firm and difficult to pass

Dehydration can also occur if a cat is suffering from diabetes or kidney problems for example

■ If a cat has been involved in a road traffic accident in the past the bones of the pelvis may have been damaged resulting in a narrowing of the pelvic canal (the space through which the bowel passes). This limits the room for faeces to pass. Overweight cats will also have extra fat in this area and be less mobile, all factors contributing to constipation

What to look for in your cat

With mild constipation you may just notice excessive digging in the litter tray with frequent, or prolonged straining, and passing only small amounts of very firm dry stool. With more severe constipation, straining can be even more excessive, with sometimes no success in passing any faeces at all. In very severe cases the cat will become more and more uncomfortable, and may also develop other signs such as being off their food and/or vomiting.

Diagnosis and treatment

Diagnosis is usually made by your veterinarian taking a careful history from you, and by examining your cat. Further investigations such as x-rays may also be necessary. Weight management will often help with constipation and in the meantime your veterinarian may advise other tactics such as maintaining good hydration and use of various laxative medications. A guide to encouraging fluid intake in cats can be found in the Free Downloads section of **www.catprofessional. com**. Pain relieving drugs for any osteoarthritis may also be

> **Blood pressure monitoring is recommended in all overweight cats, and all cats over the age of 7 years.**

required so your cat feels comfortable enough to 'go'. Make sure your litter trays are easy to access (for example on every floor of your home), clean, private and easy to use. This may mean choosing a tray with a lower side, providing a tray downstairs if usually only upstairs, and making sure it is kept away from the busy areas of the house. If you have more than one cat ensure you have enough trays – as many as you have cats plus one, placed in different locations in the home.

■ **Heart disease and high blood pressure**

In cats, there is not yet a proven link between obesity and heart disease or high blood pressure. However, the link between obesity and cardiovascular disease in people is widely accepted, and so although not proven, it is likely that being overweight will have a negative impact on the cat's heart and blood pressure. Heart disease is relatively common in middle aged cats (5-10yrs) although it can occur at any age. Obesity isn't known to cause heart disease in cats but in a cat known to have heart disease, the additional body weight in an overweight cat is certainly going to add 'strain' on the heart. High blood pressure (systemic hypertension) is common in older cats (>10 years). High blood pressure can have serious consequences, such as sudden onset blindness, and bleeding into the eye or brain. These consequences can however be prevented if the high blood pressure is picked up early and treated promptly. Blood pressure monitoring is therefore recommended in all overweight cats, and routinely in all cats over the age of 7 years.

What to look for in your cat

The most common sign that a carer may notice as a result of high blood pressure is changes in the cat's vision. This can be due to bleeding into the eye, or effects on the retina (the 'seeing layer' at the back of the eye). Vision may either just be reduced, or the cat can go suddenly completely blind. More subtle signs that carers may notice before this include restlessness, withdrawing from the family and not wanting interaction with other pets or family members, being 'grumpy', and vocalising excessively ('yowling').

The most common sign of heart disease occurs once the heart is failing and fluid builds up within or around the lungs (congestive heart failure). This results in an increased rate of breathing or breathing difficulty, with the cat working harder than they should to take a breath, or open mouth breathing ('panting').

Diagnosis and treatment

The diagnosis of high blood pressure (systemic hypertension) is made through measuring the blood pressure, using a small cuff around the leg or tail, just like it is done in people. This will often be combined with a close examination of the eyes to look for effects of the high blood pressure.

This cat has high blood pressure (hypertension) that has caused bleeding into one eye.

One sign of heart disease can be difficulty breathing, for example breathing with the mouth open (panting).

Measurement of blood pressure using a small cuff around the leg is simple and comfortable for the cat.

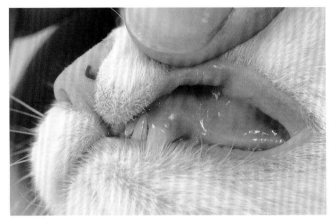

Jaundice (yellowing of the gums in this picture) is a sign of severe liver problems and can occur if an overweight cat loses weight too quickly.

Heart disease may be suspected on the basis of an examination by your veterinarian, for example, if a heart murmur (abnormal heart sound) is heard. Confirming the diagnosis usually involves a combination of x-rays and ultrasound examination.

High blood pressure can be effectively treated using daily medication. Heart disease can also be managed using combinations of medications to remove excess fluid, and improve the function of the heart, depending on the type of problem your veterinarian diagnoses.

■ Hepatic lipidosis

Hepatic lipidosis, which literally means a fatty liver, is a very serious liver condition that overweight cats are predisposed to. It can occur for a number of reasons, but most commonly occurs when overweight cats stop eating. They may stop eating because of a period of stress (e.g. a stay in a cattery), another illness that has made them feel unwell and stop eating, or due to a change in diet that they have refused to eat. The disease occurs due to alterations in their metabolism resulting in the deposition of fat within the liver causing widespread liver damage. It can occur after only a few days of inadequate food intake. Once hepatic lipidosis develops, it is a severe disease that usually requires weeks of intensive treatment and may ultimately be fatal.

It is important to be aware of this disorder, because it is always natural to think that an overweight cat can afford to go a few days without eating, and for care providers not to be concerned about this. Whereas, in fact it is more dangerous for a fat cat to go a few days without eating than it is for a thin cat. This is also why it is very important when dieting a cat, to ensure firstly that it is eating the new diet, and secondly that the weight loss is not occurring too rapidly (see **page 40, How much food should I offer my overweight cat?**).

What to look for in your cat
If your cat has not been eating well for more than 1-2 days then this warrants concern and veterinary attention. When hepatic lipidosis occurs, usually the cat will not be eating at all, may be vomiting, and will be very quiet and frequently weak. A yellow appearance (jaundice) to the skin and whites of the eyes may also be noticed.

A cat with hepatic lipidosis with a feeding tube in place. The tube passes through the skin into the stomach and is called a gastrostomy tube.

Diagnosis and treatment
Diagnosis may require a combination of bloods tests, ultrasound of the liver and collection and analysis of samples taken from the liver. Treatment involves hospitalisation (often for a prolonged period) and very intensive care by giving fluids directly into a vein (putting your cat on a drip) and placement of a feeding tube.

What causes excessive weight gain?

What is a cat's natural feeding behaviour?
In order to better understand how the way that we feed our cats influences their behaviour, and how it may sometimes lead to problems with becoming overweight, it is important to first understand the natural feeding behaviour of cats.

However much we may dislike the thought of our cute and affectionate feline friends going out and killing small mammals for food, there is no getting away from the fact that cats are specialised hunters and near the top of the food chain predators. This means that cats have evolved to be physically active, and to have to work hard for their food. If we consider a feral cat living on mice, it will typically eat about 10-20 mice over a 24 hour period. So, this also means that their bodies have been designed to eat very small meals frequently throughout the day.

For cats, both the pattern of feeding, and also the social significance of feeding is very different to that of humans. Although the lives of our domesticated cats may be somewhat different to that of their ancestors, cats retain a strong motivation

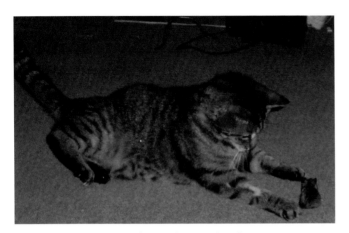

Cats in the wild expend a lot of energy chasing and catching prey.

being clever creatures then learn to manipulate this misunderstanding by their care providers, which can lead to a vicious spiral of overfeeding. We need to realise the meaning of this behaviour, and instead of rewarding it with food, we should play and interact with the cat when it is initiating social behaviour, as this is what it is really asking for.

Carers can misinterpret a cat's behaviour (rubbing, vocalising) for hunger, when the cat really wanted attention and interaction. This can easily lead to overfeeding and weight gain.

to hunt or explore to locate food, and their bodies remain designed to take in small frequent meals, throughout the day. They expend a lot of time and energy catching prey, and also playing with it prior to eating, and then given the nature of their prey they usually have to spend a significant amount of time chewing and physically consuming their food. Furthermore cats are solitary hunters, which means that they have a desire to eat alone. Unlike the situation in people, the feeding process is not a social occasion for cats!

A lack of understanding of this important difference between cat and human feeding behaviours is a common cause of misinterpretation of feline behaviours, which can lead to overfeeding. When cats exhibit behaviours such as vocalising and leg rubbing these are signs that the cat wants to initiate social behaviour, however these signs are commonly misinterpreted by carers as the cat wanting more food. Cats

What is a cat's natural diet?

In addition to the natural feeding habits of cats, we also need to think about the type of food that their bodies have been designed to survive on. Cats are obligate carnivores, which means that they must eat meat. Being such successful hunters, their bodies have never needed to evolve to be able to utilise vegetable matter and carbohydrates (starchy food) as part of their diet. Cats therefore don't have many of the metabolic pathways for processing carbohydrate diets that omnivorous species, such as dogs and humans, have.

The metabolism of cats differs from omnivores (animals that eat both meat and vegetables, like dogs and humans) in several ways:

■ Cats obtain most of their energy requirements from protein and so have a high requirement for protein

■ Cats are less able to digest and metabolise carbohydrates

■ Cats are less able to convert excess carbohydrates to a product (glycogen) that can be stored in the liver, and therefore any excess carbohydrate not used for energy will be stored as fat

■ Prolonged intake of excess carbohydrate over time can contribute to damaging the cells in the pancreas that produce insulin, and may cause diabetes

■ Cats have an essential requirement for certain amino acids (taurine, arginine, methionine, cysteine) and vitamins such as vitamin A, that are derived from animal protein in the diet

■ Cats have different essential fatty acid requirements, having a need for linolenic acid, arachidonic acid and eicosatrienoic acid to be supplied in their diets as animal protein

Wild cats would have eaten mainly small mammalian prey such as mice, rats and rabbits, as well as birds. This natural diet is high in protein, moderate in fat content and very low in carbohydrate. Furthermore, when a cat eats small prey, it is all eaten raw, and the prey is almost completely consumed – the flesh, bones and the internal organs.

What changes have occurred in the feeding behaviour and lifestyle of the modern pet cat?

Although all cats are capable of (and retain a motivation for) hunting, most domestic cats will have less opportunity to learn a wide range of hunting skills from their mother. In our modern communities there is also less prey for cats to be able to hunt. We have stepped in to remove the cats' reliance on hunting for food by providing alternative food. It is therefore our responsibility to consider the *type* of food, and the *way* that we provide food, in order to prevent any nutritional related problems.

The majority of pet cats today will have their food provided in a bowl in a single location, maybe given as two daily meals. Alternatively food may be provided ad libitum (free access to food all the time). Understanding the natural feeding behaviour of cats, it is clear that this way of providing food is far from natural for a cat. Nowadays, cats are expending less energy and time during the food consumption process.

Although most pet cats are not having to rely on hunting to obtain their food, those cats that go outdoors will still exhibit hunting behaviour, and will expend time and energy chasing things like small insects and butterflies, where there are not many small mammals to hunt.

Indoor cats

It is becoming more and more common in the modern day, for cats to be kept indoors. If these cats are not given space and opportunity to provide an outlet for their motivation to hunt (i.e. by being given opportunity for playing and jumping), it can not only result in behavioural problems, but it is inhibiting their ability to be physically active, and greatly reducing the energy they will be expending.

Misunderstanding behaviour

Furthermore, other feeding behaviours can be misinterpreted and result in over eating. For example, given that cats are designed to eat small amounts of food frequently throughout the day, it is not unusual for a cat to eat a small amount of the meal presented to it, and then walk away. This can be misinterpreted by carers that the cat doesn't like the food, and they may respond by offering something more tasty. The more palatable the food that is offered, the more likely that the cat will start to continue eating beyond the point that it is full and satisfied, and over time the sensation of feeling full becomes overridden.

Neutering

The majority of pet cats now will also be neutered. Neutering increases the risk of weight gain since the cat's energy requirements reduce by 20-25% following neutering. This is not

Neutering is important, but it does increase the risk of weight gain.

a reason to avoid neutering, as it is very important to prevent overbreeding, fighting, road accidents and a number of diseases, but carers should be aware that they will need to reduce their cats food intake following neutering to help prevent weight gain at this life stage.

What changes have occurred in the diet of the modern pet cat?

A cat's diet 60-70 years ago

If you look back in time, the majority of cats were either feral, or purely outdoor cats largely living by hunting prey. During the 1960/70s as it was becoming more popular to keep cats as pets and provide them with food, they were usually fed a mixture of table scraps, raw beef and offal (e.g. raw cow's heart and liver), and fresh rabbit. Nutritional diseases became apparent during this time due to specific nutritional deficiencies or excesses. For example:

- Nutritional secondary hyperparathyroidism: this is a disease that occurs when meat diets high in phosphate but low in calcium are fed to rapidly growing kittens, and results in very weak bones that easily break (fracture)

- Hypervitaminosis A: this is an excess of vitamin A that occurs from from feeding diets rich in liver

- Pansteatitis: this is an inflammation of fat that occurs from feeding diets high in polyunsaturated fats, e.g. certain fish, without sufficient added antioxidants

- Thiamine deficiency: this is a particular vitamin deficiency that can occur from feeding meat treated with sulphite preservatives, a completely cooked meat diet, or raw fish diet

The difference in these diets compared to a cat's natural diet is the type of meat; in the wild cats would not be eating beef, nor fish, and they would be consuming the entire small mammal to provide all the important nutrients in balanced proportions, rather than an excess of specific parts of an animal, like the liver.

The introduction of commercial diets

Commercial food was introduced in the 1970s, to provide more nutritionally balanced diets. Canned foods were based on meat, meat by-products, offal and/or fish. Extruded commercial kibble (dry food/biscuits) also became available at supermarkets and pet stores. Commonly pet cats were fed either purely canned food or a mix of canned and dry food. When you evaluate the proportion of fat, protein and carbohydrate in these diets compared to the proportion of these nutrients in small mammalian prey, which cats have evolved to live on, they are often quite different. Typically commercial foods have a much higher carbohydrate content and lower protein and fat content. When comparing wet to dry foods, on the whole dry foods also have a higher carbohydrate content when compared to a wet food of a similar type.

In the late 1980s/1990s, "Premium diets" (diets containing high quality ingredients, predominantly dry foods but also some wet foods) and "prescription diets" (specially formulated diets 'prescribed' on the recommendation of a veterinarian and designed to treat specific health problems) became increasingly available, initially only through veterinary practices, but more recently through pet stores as well. The 'premium' foods generally use high quality animal protein, typically in larger proportions than in supermarket brands, with a higher fat content. They are good quality foods and are generally exceedingly palatable to cats.

When are problems seen with modern diets?

The problem occurs when cats overeat. There may be many reasons for a cat to end up overeating, but this may occur as a result of carers inadvertently overfeeding by not following manufacturer's recommendations. This is particularly common when feeding dry foods. Cats require only small amounts of

Eating calorie dense food quickly can mean the cat is still hungry and demands more food.

these diets to meet their energy needs, and the volume of the food required is much less than care providers are accustomed to feeding with wet foods. Dry foods typically come in large bags and it is all too easy to give an extra handful here and there, without realising how many extra calories you are providing. When provided as a twice daily meal, the food is consumed quickly and the cat may not appear to be satiated, which can result in carers responding by offering more food. Furthermore, manufacturer's recommendations are often based on feeding active young cats, and so less active and older cats may be receiving too much even when the recommendations are adhered to.

How do our busy lives affect the way we feed our cats?

In our modern day busy lifestyles, it is also common for us to be in a rush and feel guilty about not spending enough time with our cats, particularly when they are seeking social interaction. I am sure that everyone can relate to those times when our cat is desperately wanting to jump on to our lap for a sleep and a cuddle and much as we would love to oblige, we simply have to get on with the housework, collect the children from school, or go to work. It is easy in these times (when those big green eyes are staring lovingly at us) to provide some more food instead, to relieve our own guilt about not having time to interact with them. Furthermore, since dry food doesn't spoil when left out, many carers will also keep a bowl of dry food out that is topped up continuously, with no real idea how much the cat is consuming each day (ad lib feeding).

Dry food is convenient to leave out for the cat to eat but this can result in over-feeding.

What are the consequences of the modern pet cat's changed lifestyle and diet?

- A generally less active lifestyle, sometimes indoor only

- Food provided to the cat without them having to expend energy to obtain it

- The type of food provided is easy to eat quickly with little effort required

- Large meals generally, and often ad libitum food given rather than feeding little and often

- Diets typically higher in carbohydrate and lower protein than the type of food that cats have evolved to live on

- A growing tendency to overfeed

When we understand and realise all of these consequences, it is not difficult to see how many of our pet cats are becoming overweight. But the good news is that all of these factors can be changed relatively easily to effectively tackle, or even better to prevent them becoming overweight.

How can weight be managed?

In theory, management of being overweight or obese is simple – we become overweight when we eat too much and don't exercise enough! The same is true for cats, so management essentially involves providing fewer calories and increasing activity. However, in practical terms, it is usually easier said than done! Breaking down each of these areas for consideration will help to provide many tips for how this can be achieved.

The following section will discuss in detail the following:

- Dietary management

- Lifestyle changes and increasing your cat's activity

1. Dietary management

Step 1: establish a baseline 'food diary'

The first step before we think about changing the way we feed or what we feed, where possible, is to very clearly calculate what and how the cat has been fed up to this point. This will enable identification of the major problem areas which need to be addressed, and will also allow calculation of the daily calorie consumption, so that a new daily calorie allowance can be set for achieving weight loss.

It is helpful for care providers to sit down with all the members of the household and to discuss keeping a very accurate feeding diary over the period of at least a week or two, PRIOR to starting any diet. It is important that all the members of the household enter anything and everything that they feed the cat during this time. This is the time to be totally honest and confess all – even if you are embarrassed that the cat enjoys treats or human food.

The details in this diary need to be as specific as possible, for example:

■ How are meals provided – frequency, amount of food and location?

■ Sachets or cans of food – brand? How many per day?

■ Dry food – brand? How much? How is this measured? Be honest here!

■ Cat treats? What type? How often?

■ Table scraps or other 'people' food? What type? How often?

■ Remember everyone in the household needs to answer these! Your cheeky cat could be getting fed multiple meals from different members of the household without you even knowing!

■ Does your cat go outside? Do they hunt? Are they known to eat elsewhere e.g. at a neighbours?

■ Is your cat on any medication? Is this given with any treats?

■ Do you have any other pets? Can your cat get access to any other petfood?

■ Does your cat tend to gorge all the food that is down at once, or nibble throughout the day?

■ How active is your cat? Do they go outdoors? Do they play with toys inside?

The veterinary staff can then go through this feeding diary and calculate your cats approximate caloric intake, as accurately as possible. This will form the basis of calculating how many calories your cat needs to be fed to achieve their goal body weight. You may be very surprised to discover just how many calories your cat is eating! The table below demonstrates the calorie content of some typical 'treats' that may be provided – if you look at how many calories your cat should be eating you will see that it doesn't take much in the way of additional treats to far exceed this!

Food type	kcal per 100g of food 'as fed'
Prawns	75
Smoked salmon	220
Haddock	105
Rump steak	125
Ham	135
Chicken breast	113
Double cream	445
Cheddar cheese	410
Cream cheese	245

Table showing calorie contents of some 'human' foods that we may use as treats. It isn't hard to see that a prawn is much better than a splash of double cream!

If George, the cat described on **page 42**, was occasionally given 30g of ham as a treat, this would provide around 40 calories – approximately a quarter of George's allocated daily calorie allowance. His carer would need to deduct a quarter of his normal diet to ensure that he still continued to lose weight.

GOAL WEIGHT – this is the initial target weight set by your veterinarian. This will not be the 'ideal' weight for your cat but a realistic step along the way. Once a goal weight is reached; another 'goal' is set until the cat weighs an ideal amount for their size.

IDEAL WEIGHT – this is the correct and healthy weight for your cat to have a normal body condition and not be overweight or obese. This weight will depend on your cat's breed and size and can be decided by your veterinarian. Generally cats weigh between 3 and 5kg but some breeds will be heavier.

Step 2: make a weight loss plan

The second step is thinking about how diet is going to be used to ensure that your cat effectively loses weight, whilst also consuming a balanced diet so that it gets all the essential nutrients that it needs, and isn't feeling hungry all of the time and making you feel guilty for not providing more food!

When we think about managing a cat's diet in order to tackle being overweight, there are 3 main aspects of diet that we need to consider:

i.   What type of food to give
ii. How much food to give
iii. How to provide the food

Type of food

It is easy to get confused about what diet we should be feeding with the vast array of different cat foods that are available in supermarkets and pet food shops, let alone in the veterinary clinics as well.

In addition to choices in different brands of foods, we have choice between wet (canned/sachets/trays) diets and dry (biscuits) diets, complete and complementary foods, diets designed for 'junior' cats, 'senior' cats, 'indoor' cats, 'neutered' cats, 'hairball' diets, 'light' diets, 'sensitive stomach' diets, and even diets designed for different breeds of cats. These are all diets that may be available at supermarkets, pet shops or through your veterinary clinic. It can be difficult to choose an appropriate diet for your cat without getting the best advice, and without having an understanding of the differences between the various types of diets.

There are also many different considerations to take into account when choosing the best diet for your cat, and this is just one of the aspects where the veterinary team become important in being able to give the best advice about which of these diets to choose. Don't be afraid to ask your veterinarian for dietary advice, even if you aren't buying your diet through the veterinary practice.

A few general points to remember with different food types include:

- A higher protein – lower carbohydrate diet is most appropriate for weight reduction – look at the packages for comparisons. It is not a requirement for manufacturers to list the carbohydrate contents however, and therefore sometimes the companies need to be contacted to obtain this information, or the levels calculated from the other listed ingredients

- The majority of calories should be provided in the form of a 'complete' diet (whether the diet is complete or complementary should be stated on the packaging. Complete diets contain all the cats required nutrients in a balanced form)

- Wet foods tend to be lower in carbohydrate than dry foods

- With dry foods the same calories are provided in a much smaller volume of food compared to wet foods

- It is easy to overfeed dry food – required amounts need to be accurately measured with no extra given, this means weighing on kitchen scales. A cup or jug is sometimes provided with food to enable the correct amount to be measured out, however measuring the food in this way is not accurate enough when weight loss is required

- Whenever treats are given these must be taken out of the total daily calorie allowance, i.e. the more treats, the less of the main diet is fed and bear in mind this could lead to nutritional deficiencies as the cat is eating less of the complete diet

Dry food contains more calories per gram than wet food. The portions in this picture have the same amount of calories.

■ When feeding dry food, whether as part or all of the diet, think about how it is fed. Consider making the eating process slower and more challenging – for example by offering food in feed balls, or puzzle feeders (see **pages 39, 45-46**). These help to slow down consumption and increase activity

Some additional general dietary advice is given at the end of this section under '**Avoiding weight gain**' (**pages 54-55**). Really once your cat has become overweight, even a calorie restricted 'light' diet that you can buy over the counter probably isn't going to be enough to successfully achieve weight loss. A specially formulated veterinary prescription diet is going to be required, as these diets are specially formulated to be successful in safely achieving weight loss in overweight cats, without risking causing other health complications. Although these diets can be obtained from the internet, they should be prescribed by your veterinarian and need to be fed under their guidance.

If your cat is only mildly overweight, or there is another reason that you are unable take your cat to the veterinarian, or for them to undertake a diet under veterinary guidance, then the next best thing is to follow all the other advice in this book and use an over the counter calorie restricted 'light' diet. Or if your cat has been severely overfed, then simply cutting down to the recommended amount, cutting out treats and increasing activity may be effective. However it must be emphasised that if you do simply cut back on your cat's normal food then you risk feeding less of the vital nutrients at the same time as reducing the calorie intake compared to the specially formulated veterinary prescription which will be more effective. The weight loss will also be achieved more safely with these special diets and so they should be your first choice.

There is often the perception that veterinary prescription diets are more expensive than diets bought from the supermarket. However, when being fed in the correct amounts, they can actually work out cheaper than some poorer quality diets available in the supermarket.

When it comes to veterinary prescription diets, there are generally two different types of diets that have been designed for weight loss:

- High fibre, low fat diets

- High protein, low carbohydrate diets

These specially formulated diets also contain other useful substances such as L-carnitine, which increases the conversion

A puzzle feeder is a good way to make feeding dry food more interesting for your cat.

of fat to energy, resulting in more effective weight loss while helping to maintain lean body mass (muscle). Both of these prescription diets come in wet (canned/trays/pouches) and dry versions. The canned versions will always contain slightly lower proportions of carbohydrates than the dry versions, and a larger volume of food will be able to be fed with the canned formulations.

How do high fibre, low fat diets work?
High fibre low fat diets were the diets more traditionally designed for weight loss. This is a similar type of composition to the type of diet we might use ourselves if we were trying to lose weight. However, as you will have learnt at the beginning of this section, cats use nutrients differently to omnivores like dogs and

people, and this means that their requirements for weight reduction also differ, reflecting their inability to metabolise and store excessive carbohydrate in the liver, but only store it as fat. Feeding a high fibre low fat diet will be successful in achieving weight loss but there can be several problems with achieving weight loss in this way:

- the weight loss tends to occur at the expense of lean body mass (muscle)

- the metabolic rate (the rate food is broken down and used) may be lowered, which will predispose to regaining the weight

- these diets may be unpalatable to some cats

- increasing fibre can reduce the digestibility of the diet's nutrients

- larger volumes of faeces will be produced

One of the big benefits of these diets is that a comparatively large volume of food can be fed whilst still only providing limited calories, so if you have a very greedy cat that is accustomed to eating large volumes of food, then this could be the right diet to choose for them.

How does a low carbohydrate, high protein diet work?
In more recent years, as it has become more recognised and understood that cats are better suited to a higher protein, lower carbohydrate diet, it has also been recognised that this type of diet is an excellent diet for achieving weight loss by altering the cat's metabolism. This is the same type of specially formulated prescription diet recommended for cats with diabetes. This diet is effective at achieving weight loss in cats whilst maintaining their muscle mass better than a high fibre low fat diet would. The additional benefits of this diet above a high fibre low fat diet are that it is more palatable, and smaller volumes of faeces will be produced. However it is important that the amount of this food given is tightly regulated. These diets can actually be quite high in calories and so it is vital that the amount of food provided is carefully calculated.

How much food should I offer my overweight cat?
When it comes to working out how much food to give, there are a few calculations that need to be made. The information obtained from these can be used to work out how much food (weight and/or volume) your cat should be given at the start of their weight loss programme. The maths might seem intimidating but this is where your veterinarian/veterinary nurse can help.

You need to know:

1. Your cat's accurate weight

2. Your cat's estimated 'ideal' weight (the healthy weight for your cat, taking into account size, breed and age)

Your veterinarian can advise you on the best weight-loss diet for your cat.

3. Your cat's 'goal' weight (an initial 'target' on the journey to the ideal weight)

4. Current calorie intake

5. Calories needed to maintain ideal weight

6. Calories needed to achieve gradual weight loss

7. Calorie content of chosen diet(s)

It is important to obtain an accurate weight for your cat. As far as possible, the same scales should be used for monitoring your cat's weight to avoid any inaccuracies with variations between different sets of scales. Your veterinarian will estimate what your cat's 'ideal' body weight should be. Cats vary quite significantly in size and every cat is different. For the average cat, most of them will have an ideal weight somewhere between 3.5-5kg, but your veterinarian will estimate this more accurately based on their breed, skeletal size and current weight and body condition score. A cat's body weight at about one year of age is usually about what their ideal weight should be, since they are fully grown at that stage but usually not overweight. Once the ideal weight has been estimated, then the first 'goal' weight will be set. This is to help achieve a good rate of weight loss over a period of time. Once the first 'goal' weight has been reached, then another 'goal' weight will be set, until eventually the 'ideal' weight is reached. Management is aiming at achieving a loss of 1% in bodyweight per week. Care should be taken that weight loss does not exceed 1.3% per week.

As a rule of thumb, in order to lose weight, a cat needs 60-70% of the calories required to maintain their ideal weight. The calories that a cat needs to maintain its 'ideal' body weight can be calculated using the equation:

Calories per day (kcal) = (30 x bodyweight in kg) + 70

This can be simplified to about 40-50 kcal per kg bodyweight per day (40kcal per kg for less active cats and 50kcal per kg for more active cats).

In cats that have been severely overeating however, this could result in reducing their food intake too quickly and leading to too rapid weight loss. If you have managed to keep a good food diary, this is where it is used to calculate the current calorie

intake. This can then be used further as a guide for calculating how many calories to start your cat off on to achieve a good but safe rate of weight loss.

This is a good starting point, but every cat will be different, and so it is important that weight is monitored closely, and the amount of food adjusted depending on whether weight loss is occurring too quickly or too slowly, when compared to the 'goal' weights that have been set.

Remember to accurately weigh out the required amount of dry food. An extra 10 biscuits a day may seem insignificant and go unnoticed when measuring the food out into a container, but this extra food will contain a significant amount of calories!

Case Example: 'George'

- George weighs 6.5kg, and his ideal weight is estimated to be 5.5kg.

- If we aim for 1% loss in body weight per week, this works out as 0.065kg (65g) per week

- We would set the first 'goal' weight at one month, so this would be 6.25kg if we are successful in losing 1% bodyweight each week

- So, we would be looking at it taking approximately 4 months to achieve the 'ideal' weight – and this is if everything goes to plan! In reality it is normal for safe weight loss to take longer

To calculate how many calories George needs each day, we use the equation mentioned above ((30 x ideal BW) + 70), so this equals (30 x 5.5) + 70 = 235kcal/day – this is the calories required to maintain his ideal bodyweight.

George needs to lose weight, so we need to feed him 60-70% of this amount, which calculates to be 141-165 kcal per day.

George has been put onto a canned food that contains 200kcal per 170g tin, so he needs to be fed a total of 3/4 tin daily (=150kcal).

The equivalent type of food in dry formulation contains 350kcal per 100g of food, so if he was fed purely dry food he would need about 43g (150kcal) of dry food daily.

Or he could be fed 50:50 wet and dry food, providing half the amount of both the calculated rations.

How to provide the food

Taking into consideration all of the factors discussed earlier in this section, the *way* that food is provided is as important as the *type* of food that is fed. However, before you change the way that your cat is fed too dramatically, it is important to successfully change the diet and be sure that your cat is eating it, rather than changing too much at once.

Changing the diet

One of the problems with managing an overweight cat, is having to change it onto a different diet. Although overweight cats are usually perceived to be greedy, they can actually also be fussy in the type of food they will eat, particularly if they have become accustomed to eating a very palatable diet. This part of a diet can be the most worrying for a carer – will their cat eat a new, lower calorie diet?

It is also very dangerous for an overweight cat to suddenly stop eating, and lose weight too quickly, predominantly due to the risk of developing hepatic lipidosis (see **page 27**). Therefore any change in diet needs to be managed very carefully.

Changing cats from a purely dry diet to a wet diet can be particularly problematic, especially when a cat has become accustomed to eating dry food only. A change in diet is best done when the cat is feeling well, so if the cat has been experiencing any health problems, these should ideally be resolved or at least improved, prior to attempting the change onto a weight control diet.

It is important to accurately weigh dry food; a few extra biscuits can contain many calories.

Some cats are easier to change onto a different diet than others. If you are lucky your cat will eat the diet straight away. So, this is the first thing to try. If your cat likes the new diet straight away, then wean it onto this over a period of a few days to avoid any stomach upsets – for example:

- Day 1: 75% old diet, 25% new diet

- Day 2: 50% old diet, 50% new diet

- Day 3: 25% old diet, 75% new diet

- Day 4 onwards: 100% new diet

If your cat doesn't immediately like the new diet, a few different tricks can be tried:

- Offer the new diet in a container that is the same as was used for the old diet and place the new diet next to the old diet. Offer fresh new diet at each feeding. Once the cat starts to eat a little as it becomes familiar with it, gradually reduce the quantity of the old diet by a small amount each day, aiming to completely change the diet over 1-2 weeks

- If food is usually left out all of the time, change this to only leaving the food out for about an hour, and removing any uneaten food after an hour. Once the new feeding regime has been accepted, then start weaning onto the new diet as described above

- Initially mix small quantities of your cat's favourite food to the new food (but remember this is only in the initial stages – otherwise these calories must be counted in the total daily requirement)

- Make sure your cat is in a quiet environment with no distractions when you are offering the food

Once you have managed to successfully change your cat onto the weight loss diet, then you can think about how to provide the diet. As far as possible we should try to mimic a cat's natural feeding behaviour, so all of the factors discussed on **pages 28 and 29** apply such as offering small amounts often, in different locations, and encouraging the cat to expend energy to obtain the food.

This can be done by simply providing small amounts of food in different locations in the house so that the cat has to walk around and look for the food. Spread out the daily ration into small frequent meals throughout the day.

If you are out all day, and putting the food in different locations doesn't slow down your cat's food consumption adequately, then the use of feed timers can sometimes be helpful too. They can be set to 'remove the lid from the food' at specific times, only allowing access to each meal at the designated time.

When dry food is used, there are a whole variety of ways that this can be fed to make feeding a more challenging and active process:

- Treat balls: put part of the day's biscuit allocation in the ball and allow the cat to push the ball around to release the treats. These are available from most pet shops and veterinary practices

- Provide individual biscuits in a variety of locations around the house. This can include use of 3 dimensional spaces to make the cat climb or jump to get to them (e.g. on stairs, tops of scratching trees/posts). Note that if your cat is very overweight or suffering from osteoarthritis they may be unable to jump up (or this may risk severe harm if the very overweight cat falls) meaning that these techniques cannot be used. Hopefully the exercise and play challenges can be increased in all cats as weight loss occurs

Food timers can help to spread out food consumption over the day when carers are out for long periods.

Treat balls can make finding food more challenging.

■ When your cat has become accustomed to these other ways of being fed, then you can make obtaining food even more challenging (and fun):

– There are various commercially available 'puzzle feeders' of varying complexities in design, but they all aim to give the cat some challenges in getting food e.g. having to fish individual biscuits out from a small hole

– Toilet roll tube pyramids – this form of puzzle feeder can be simply and cheaply made by gluing cardboard toilet roll tubes together to form a pyramid, and attaching the base to a piece of wood or carpet tile to provide stability – place a biscuit half way along each tube so that the cat needs to retrieve each biscuit one at a time, using its paw

– Placing biscuits inside cardboard boxes, egg boxes, paper bags or a rolled up piece of paper

– Throw biscuits, one at a time, across the floor, or up the stairs, allowing the cat to retrieve each one before throwing the next. Some cats will really enjoy chasing biscuits as they are thrown and this will greatly increase their physical activity too

2. Lifestyle changes and increasing your cat's activity

Using some of the above feeding methods will in itself greatly

A puzzle feeder with 2 inquisitive cats.

A simple and inexpensive way of making finding food more interesting.

increase your cat's activity by forcing them to expend more energy to obtain their food.

In addition to this, activity can be increased in other ways too. Although you may work long hours, try to allocate even just 5-10 minutes a day to play with your cat to get them moving and exercising each day. Even just 5 minutes of playing twice a day will make a big difference. Cats particularly enjoy predatory play, such as using fishing rod type toys and retrieval games. Remember not to use your hands or feet as targets as this can become a habit leading to unexpected attacks!

Provide your cat with interesting toys and items to explore such as:

- Catnip toys, particularly placed in high up locations or tops of stairs to encourage the lazy feline to have to exercise to investigate

- Rolled or scrunched up piece of paper

- A cork

- Ping pong balls – for example these can be placed inside an empty cardboard box, or the bath tub to allow the cat to bat them around without getting them wedged under the sofa straightaway!

- Paper bags (with handles removed) make a popular toy

An active cat is a healthy cat and most cats love to chase a fishing toy.

■ Cardboard boxes

■ Provide high resting places in the home – cats are natural climbers – encourage use of tall scratching posts, shelving, high furniture

Remember that novel items will always stimulate more interest, so it is important to keep changing the toys and other items of environmental enrichment in order to maintain the cat's interest and desire to explore new things. This doesn't mean having to buy new toys every week, but you may want to keep a box of toys hidden away and rotate each week which ones are given to your cat.

Grooming your cat can also be an enjoyable activity for both cat and carer, and one that can help develop the bond with your cat.

If your cat is in a household with other cats, consider whether any conflict, or dislike of the other cats may be contributing towards inactivity, for example if the cat spends most of it's time hiding from the other cat(s). If this is the case, professional advice from a pet behaviour counsellor may need to be sought (discuss this with your veterinarian).

> **Even just short periods of play (just 5-10 minutes) every day will get your cat moving, help them lose weight and improve their quality of life.**

A climbing frame can increase activity and make an indoor cat's life more interesting.

For cats that are kept solely indoors, there are a range of things that can be done to enrich their environment further and encourage activity. In some situations outdoor enclosures can also be bought or made and this provision of fresh air and a very interesting environment will encourage exploration. Gardens and yards can be fenced to prevent your cat exploring any further, yet allow them the outdoor space to move around. The Indoor Cat Initiative run by the Ohio State University provides a wealth of further information on how to enrich the life of an indoor cat. Please see the **further information** section on **page 72** for more details.

Finally, don't forget that when your cat is looking at you vocalising, or rubbing against you, they may well be asking for social interaction and not food. So, next time this happens, refrain from topping up the food bowl and reach for a toy, or grooming brush instead.

What check-ups are needed when assessing weight loss?
So, the calculations are completed and the diet chosen, you feel confident and know how much to feed. However, that is not the end of the story, but just the beginning and monitoring during a weight loss programme is very important.

When your cat is overweight, there are two main areas of consideration with regard to monitoring:

■ Weight and body condition score monitoring

■ Monitoring for illnesses and other problems associated with being overweight

The guidelines your veterinarian will give you about how much to feed at the beginning of a weight loss programme is just a starting point. Every cat is different, and requires regular review of their health, body condition score and weight. The aim is for them to lose 1% of their bodyweight each week. If weight loss is not occurring quickly enough, or occurring too quickly then the diet needs to be reviewed. Weighing once every 1-2 weeks is important at the start of the diet, to ensure that weight loss isn't occurring too quickly. Contact your veterinary practice immediately if your cat is not interested in the new diet, stops eating, or seems at all unwell during the weight loss programme. Once a steady rate of weight loss is occurring and your cat is eating the new diet well, then once a month weighing is adequate. Each month, weight and body condition score should be reviewed and a new target weight set for the next month. The diet should be adjusted as required, depending on the amount of weight loss achieved in the previous one month period. See **Section 3** for how your veterinary practice can help you achieve these targets.

As discussed earlier in this section, being overweight can result in a number of illnesses, or aggravate other existing conditions. The illnesses associated with being overweight, and what to look out for in your cat are discussed on **pages 19-28**. If there is any concern that a cat is suffering from a weight related condition, then following an examination by your veterinarian, further

Weight monitoring is important to ensure that your cat is losing weight successfully, at an acceptable rate, and not losing weight too quickly.

investigations may be advised, such as blood tests for diabetes or x-rays for osteoarthritis.

What challenges might I face when dieting an overweight cat?

There is no doubt that starting a weight loss plan for your cat is a challenge. You may have certain specific concerns such as those discussed below. Remember you are not alone in having these concerns, many carers do, and weight loss can be a rocky road for many cats and their care providers. However, with your motivation and help from your veterinary practice, most, if not all, problems can be overcome.

■ **I've got other cats that aren't overweight, how do I feed the other cats without overfeeding the overweight one?**

It is not unusual for a house to be home to an overweight cat and a slim cat. Therefore sticking to a special diet for one and not another can be very difficult. It is worth asking your veterinarian or nurse if the slimmer cat can eat the specific weight loss food. If it is not harmful to the slimmer cat (which it is unlikely to be) then both can be fed the same food, with the slimmer cat being fed extra food between meals, or a higher volume of the diet food. Other methods include limiting the access of the fatter cat to a feeding area using magnetic or microchip cat flaps. Although this can be an expensive option, it can be very effective, as the slimmer cat can continue to have ad lib food access. An alternative is providing the thin cats food inside a box, with the only access being through a small hole that the overweight cat cannot fit through (but care needs to be taken that the overweight cat cannot try to get through and get stuck which could cause injury). However, if these options are not possible, most cats will adjust to portion feeding instead of 'ad lib' feeding with the slimmer cat being offered a larger portion at each meal, and the cats being kept separate at feeding time. Remember that eating is not a social occasion for cats, they don't need to be together when eating, and in fact will probably prefer having their own quiet place to eat.

■ **Are there any problems associated with dieting cats?**

Potentially yes, this is why close contact with your veterinary practice and close supervision is important. As has been mentioned earlier in this chapter some potential problems can arise from too rapid weight loss.

This is why dieting a cat must be closely supervised and the amount of food and therefore calories carefully calculated. Contact your veterinary practice immediately if your cat stops eating, or refuses a new diet.

■ **How long will it take for my cat to lose enough weight?**

Weight loss in cats should never be rushed. As mentioned earlier in this book slow and steady is the right way. Imagine it to be like a marathon, not a sprint! Rapid weight loss can cause serious health problems. So you are going to need to be patient. Although seeing a large drop in the number on the

> **An overweight cat should lose 1% (maximum 1.3%) of their bodyweight each week. If weight loss is too rapid, then hepatic lipidosis can develop (see page 27).**

scales each week may sound good, it is not the best thing for your cat.

Slow weight loss can be frustrating and make us want to give up and revert to the old diet that seemed to make them happy. But remember, in the long term losing weight will prolong and improve your cat's life so stick with it.

■ **What if my cat still isn't losing weight?**

This is the really frustrating bit. You stick to the diet, play with your cat every day when you come home from work (although all you want to do is put your feet up) and yet the scales are showing the same number. If your cat isn't losing weight the next step is to contact your veterinary practice. They can check your cat over and make sure no health problems have been missed that might be having an effect. They can also review the amount of food you are feeding. Here comes the difficult bit – you need to be totally honest and this is why the food diary is really helpful. Calories can sneak into your cat's diet and sabotage your cat's weight loss

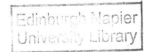

unintentionally. So ask yourself if any extras have been eaten, for example:

- Milk – cat milk and cow's milk contain extra calories
- Treats – the odd one won't hurt will it? Yes it can do! Ask your veterinarian or nurse for advice on using part of the daily food portion as treats whilst trying to find other ways to interact and bond with your cat such as play. See the table on **page 36** that illustrates the calorie content of some favourite treats.
- Human food – does your cat hang around under the high chair or lick the cream cheese off the knife in the dishwasher? This all adds to calories eaten.
- Somebody else feeding your cat – this could be a neighbour (as discussed below and opposite) or a family member who isn't sure how much the cat is allowed to eat, or a friendly child who likes feeding the cat.

If you can answer 'no' to all of these points then your veterinarian may need to review the diet and make some adjustments, and you may need to work even harder at encouraging your cat to be more active.

■ My cat eats elsewhere and hunts so what can I do?

A severely obese cat could take over a year to reach their target weight.

The clever cat put on a diet may realise that entering next doors cat flap and eating their cat's food is a simple way to supplement their diet. To help avoid this you can do a number of things:

- Speak to your neighbours – find out where your cat is going. It is likely that your neighbours are not too pleased about your cats thieving ways either. Perhaps you could keep your cat indoors at the time they feed their cat? Perhaps they could improve their 'security' by using a microchip or magnetic cat flap and gently 'shoo' your cat away if they see them. It is possible your neighbours like your cat and are feeding them willingly. If so then politely ask them to stop, explaining it is for your cat's health, or provide them with a portion of your cat's food allowance so they can continue to offer the occasional treat.

> **If neighbours are over-feeding your cat explain why the diet is so important and provide them with a portion of the daily food allowance to give as treats.**

Remember to deduct this from your cat's daily allowance so that you are not over-feeding them. It may be that the neighbours can become involved in the weight loss process, and by communicating with them how much your cat needs to lose, they may be able to help, and support the process.

- If you don't see your neighbours, you could write them a note 'from the cat' explaining why it's really important that they're not fed however cute they are and however much they appear to be hungry!
- If you do not know who is feeding your cat you can buy brightly coloured collars that you can write a message on, such as 'on a diet, please do not feed me'.

Where present, hunting is an unpleasant feature of cat ownership. Actually it is unusual for a prolific hunter to be overweight, as they expend a lot of energy catching their prey, and usually spend a lot of time outdoors. However, occasionally hunting cats eat all of their prey and gain weight. A few cats are such effective hunters that food intake inside has to be adjusted accordingly, but this risks increasing the hunter's activities even more. A few of the following techniques can reduce hunting:

- Keep your cat indoors at dawn and dusk (preferably overnight) as these times are associated with most mouse and other small rodent hunting activity.
- Put a bell on your cat's collar. Clever hunters will adjust their technique and continue to hunt but it may help warn the victims in time.
- Provide lots of opportunity to play indoors, particularly using that hunting technique of stalking a moving object and pouncing. Fishing rod and wand toys are good for this, or even a fluffy toy or feathers on a string pulled along the ground. Laser pointers can also be popular with cats but make sure you avoid pointing them into their eyes and only use these indoors and away from windows.

■ My cats are indoor cats and I work long hours, how can I increase their activity?

There is no doubt that being an indoor cat means you are more likely to gain weight through moving less. When busy and out a lot of the day, we as carers feel we have no choice but to fill the bowl so that our cat is not hungry whilst we are out. However, this constant access to food and temptation to spend all day grooming or asleep can result in weight gain. The first thing to ask your veterinarian about is the type of food you are giving so that you can calculate the amount of food your cat should be offered each day. As mentioned earlier in this section, timed feeders can be used to prevent a cat eating all of the day's food at once and then being hungry. Combined with the correct diet and calories eaten you need to get lazy cats out of bed and off the sofa more often! It is important to provide an interesting environment for indoor

Remember a very overweight inactive cat will not be able to suddenly cope with half an hour of chasing a fishing toy, but the time needs to be steadily built up as their fitness improves. Initially just 5 minutes a day of playing will make a difference.

- Preventing unwanted kittens

- Preventing certain types of cancer and other illnesses. For example, pyometra (an accumulation of pus in the womb) which can be a problem in unneutered female cats

- Avoiding the behavioural problems of unneutered cats such as urine marking in the home, 'calling' behaviour and wandering

- Reducing the risk of road traffic accidents which are more common in cats that wander further from their home

- Reducing the risks of fighting and transmission of bacterial and viral infections. For example feline leukaemia and immunodeficiency viruses can both be spread by a bite from an infected cat

cats so they don't become bored, and anything that stimulates their interest for exploring, playing and jumping will increase their activity levels. A range of tips for increasing activity and reducing boredom are given on **pages 46-48**

Avoiding weight gain – what can be done to prevent weight gain and maintain a healthy body weight?

We have discussed so far the causes of excess weight gain and ways to manage it. However, it would obviously be preferable to avoid a cat from becoming overweight in the first place. Furthermore, once your overweight cat has successfully reached its ideal bodyweight, you want to ensure that the weight doesn't start creeping back on again!

Some of the factors that contribute to weight gain cannot be avoided. Neutering your cat is recommended as this has multiple beneficial effects including:

For many of the reasons outlined above, an unneutered cat often doesn't make as good a pet.

After neutering, a cat needs less calories to live a normal life. Therefore after neutering it is important to choose a suitable diet and feeding regime to prevent weight gain in later life. Your veterinary practice will be able to help advise you in this respect.

To prevent your cat gaining extra weight the following should be considered:

- Reduce the number of calories offered to a recently neutered cat, and keep an extra close eye on their weight and body condition score. Body condition score can be more useful than simply weighing your cat, particularly for young growing cats after neutering, as they will not have reached their adult ideal weight. If you are concerned your cat is gaining too much weight, consult your veterinarian

■ Be prepared to adjust the type and amount of food offered as necessary, as soon as a bit of extra weight gain is noticed. This may simply involve cutting down on treats, slightly reducing the amount of food offered or feeding a calorie restricted diet, such as a 'light' diet, or a diet designed for neutered cats. Your veterinary practice will be able to advise you regarding this

■ Increase activity (particularly important in indoor cats), as discussed on **pages 46-48**. Playing with your cat can also improve their quality of life and bonding with you as their carer

■ Carefully consider the type of food given, and the way that it is given, as discussed on **pages 37-46**, for example weighing the food rather than providing an unlimited amount and offering it in different locations

■ Accurately calculate calorie requirements and stick to only feeding the calculated amounts

■ Limit treats to part of the daily calorie requirement rather than offering these as 'extras'

■ Weigh dry food accurately

■ Regularly monitor your cat's body condition score and general health via health checks at your veterinary practice and monitoring of your cat yourself at home. This is particularly important for cats that have successfully lost weight – don't allow the weight to creep on again, keep in touch with your veterinary practice

■ Act quickly – if you feel your cat is gaining weight seek veterinary advice as soon as possible before it becomes a problem

> **After neutering regular checks of weight and body condition score are important to identify weight gain before the cat becomes overweight.**

Optimal weight loss planner

Adapted with kind permission of Prof Juergen Zentek

Example	
Overweight cat:	**6kg starting weight**
Target weight:	**5kg**
Expected weight loss period:	**18 weeks**

Weeks required to reach a target weight (based on 1% weight loss per week*)

Starting weight (kg)	1	2	3	4	5	6	7	8	9	10	11	12	13	14	15	16	17	18	19	20
10	9.9	9.8	9.7	9.6	9.5	9.4	9.3	9.2	9.1	9.0	9.0	8.9	8.8	8.7	8.6	8.5	8.4	8.3	8.3	8.2
9.0	8.9	8.8	8.7	8.6	8.6	8.5	8.4	8.3	8.2	8.1	8.1	8.0	7.9	7.8	7.7	7.7	7.6	7.5	7.4	7.4
8.0	7.9	7.8	7.8	7.7	7.6	7.5	7.5	7.4	7.3	7.2	7.2	7.1	7.0	6.9	5.9	6.8	6.7	6.7	6.6	6.5
7.5	7.4	7.4	7.3	7.2	7.1	7.1	7.0	6.9	6.9	6.8	6.7	6.6	6.6	6.5	6.5	6.4	6.3	6.3	6.2	6.1
7	6.9	6.9	6.8	6.7	6.7	6.6	6.5	6.5	6.4	6.3	6.3	6.2	6.1	6.1	6.0	6.0	5.9	5.8	5.8	5.7
6.5	6.4	6.4	6.3	6.2	6.2	6.1	6.1	6.0	5.9	5.9	5.8	5.8	5.7	5.6	5.6	5.5	5.5	5.4	5.4	5.3
6	5.9	5.9	5.8	5.8	5.7	5.6	5.6	5.5	5.5	5.4	5.4	5.3	5.3	5.2	5.2	5.1	5.1	5.0	5.0	4.9
5.5	5.4	5.4	5.3	5.3	5.2	5.2	5.1	5.1	5.0	5.0	4.9	4.9	4.8	4.8	4.7	4.7	4.6	4.6	4.5	4.5
5	5.0	4.9	4.9	4.8	4.8	4.7	4.7	4.6	4.6	4.5	4.5	4.4	4.4	4.3	4.3	4.3	4.2	4.2	4.1	4.1
4.5	4.5	4.4	4.4	4.3	4.3	4.2	4.2	4.2	4.1	4.1	4.0	4.0	3.9	3.9	3.9	3.8	3.8	3.8	3.7	3.7
4.0	4.0	3.9	3.9	3.8	3.8	3.8	3.7	3.7	3.7	3.6	3.6	3.5	3.5	3.5	3.4	3.4	3.4	3.3	3.3	3.3

* weight loss may vary according to the individual cat.

If you suspect your cat is overweight or obese, after reading the first two sections of this book you may be keen to start your cat on a weight loss programme today. As has been discussed, there are a number of potential health problems associated with being overweight. However, this is not something to rush into, it is important to plan weight loss carefully to maximise success and minimise problems. So before rushing off to buy a special type of food it is worth visiting your veterinary practice. They can help you and your cat in a number of ways that we will discuss in this section.

So make an appointment, initially with your veterinarian for a good chat about your concerns. Even if you haven't taken your cat to the veterinarian before (or only very infrequently) don't worry, now is the time to start.

A good relationship with your veterinarian is very important. You should feel able to discuss your concerns openly. Your veterinarian is the best person to advise you on how to put your cat onto a weight loss diet. You should feel able to ask your veterinarian or veterinary nurse any questions and they should be able to answer you clearly in a way you can understand.

If you feel that the relationship you have with your veterinarian or veterinary nurse is not answering all your concerns then you can ask to see another veterinarian within the practice, or look for another practice. Do not feel uncomfortable doing this – it is within your rights to choose the veterinarian you feel is best suited to look after your cat and your previous veterinarian will understand this. It is worth asking if anyone within the practice has a special interest in cats

The UK cat charity, the Feline Advisory Bureau, has a list of vet practices (mainly in the UK) that are members of the charity (see **http://www.fabcats.org/owners/choosing_a_vet/index.php**) which is a good indication of enthusiasm and knowledge in feline medicine. The American Association of Practitioners also has an online directory of member practices at **http://www.catvets.com/findadoctor/findadoctor.aspx**.

A number of feline-only practices exist in many countries and you may be fortunate in finding one of these in your area.

Veterinarians specialising in feline medicine can be contacted by your veterinarian for further advice, if needed, or referral to a specialist can be arranged.

> **Remember that it is very difficult to follow a diet plan, there may be set-backs and you will probably appreciate support and advice along the way. Just as people on diets rely on support groups, so can you and your cat!**

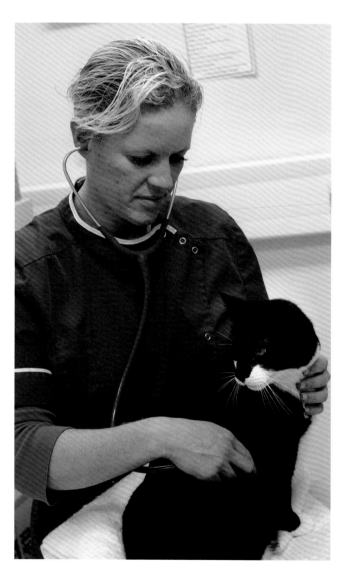

What information might my veterinarian need to know?

Before going for your appointment have a think about what your veterinarian may ask you and maybe even jot down some of the following information as it is easy to forget to mention something during the consultation that you think of later. In **Section 2** we discussed what information needed to be considered before starting a diet. In the box below are some relevant questions and a few more your veterinarian may need the answers to when thinking about a diet plan. It is also relevant to consider the relationship between your overweight cat and any other cats in your household. We may not always be aware of it, but cats can feel very stressed and intimidated by other cats that they share a house with, even though they may not overtly show signs of this. However, inactivity can be one sign of stress in a multi-cat household. Some cats may also undergo 'emotional eating', a little bit like we may 'comfort eat' if we are stressed about something!

- What type of food does your cat eat?
- How much do they eat each day? Either weigh the food or approximate, e.g. how many sachets, handfuls of dry food
- What treats do you give and how many per day? Be honest! Any human food?
- Does your cat drink milk?
- When is your cat fed (how often and at what times)?

- Where in the house is your cat fed?
- Does your cat hunt?
- Does your cat eat elsewhere e.g. neighbours house?
- Does your cat nibble food slowly or eat the entire portion at once?
- Do you have other pets and what is your cat's relationship with them?
- What is your cat's activity level – does he/she go outside? Does he/she play?
- Do you feel your cat is under stress of any form e.g. from neighbouring cats, other cats in the household, or a new baby for example?
- Do you have any other health concerns about your cat? Remember to mention anything that concerns you –
  - Has he/she been drinking more or urinating more?
  - Is he/she having trouble going to the toilet? Any sign of discomfort passing urine or faeces?
  - Does he/she suffer any vomiting/diarrhoea?
  - Is he/she more lethargic than normal?
  - Does he/she move around normally i.e. climbing the stair easily or is there any sign of stiffness or discomfort moving around?
  - Have you noticed that the coat is looking dull, scurfy and unkempt – ie is he/she grooming less?

A blood sample may be needed if your veterinarian suspects a health problem.

At the consultation your veterinarian may also want to do the following:

- Check your cat over for any health problems, including those associated with being overweight, but also any other issues that may affect the weight loss programme. Blood pressure measurement is recommended in overweight cats and all cats over the age of 7 years

- Weigh your cat and assess their body condition score to provide a 'starting point' and advise you on the target weight that would be healthy for your cat

- Your veterinarian may recommend that further investigations are performed before starting a diet. For example, if diabetes mellitus is suspected as a complication of your cat's weight, analysis of blood and/or urine samples may be recommended.

A diagnosis of diabetes influences the type of diet offered and treatment and monitoring recommendations

Your veterinarian can then advise on and if necessary provide a diet suitable for your cat, and advise you on the amount to feed. The calculations discussed in **Section 2** may seem complicated but your veterinarian or veterinary nurse will be more familiar with working out calories required and used to advising carers of overweight cats.

If any health problems are discovered then treatment can be discussed. This is an opportunity to air any concerns you might have about the weight loss programme. Don't worry about mentioning anything – they will have managed many overweight cats before and will understand any reservations you have. If you would feel more comfortable chatting to a veterinary nurse then ask for an appointment, they will be happy to have a chat and listen to your worries, sometimes they have a little more time than the veterinarian, with longer consultations. A lot of veterinary staff (the majority!) are pet owners and so know all about the problems of feeding our pets. Some of us have a fat cat of our own!

How do weight loss clinics work?

People on diets can really benefit from support during their weight loss programme, and they tend to be more successful at losing weight if they take part in meetings. The same may be true for cats and hopefully your veterinary practice can offer you further appointments at a weight loss clinic. This may be run by a veterinarian or a nurse at the practice. If your practice does not

run a specific weight loss clinic, it is worth asking if you can visit the veterinarian or the nurse at intervals during your cat's diet to weigh them, assess progress and address any problems that have arisen.

Weight loss clinics

Monitoring during weight management has been discussed on **page 49**, and this is a key area for you to be working with your veterinary practice team. It is advisable that your cat is weighed every month during the weight loss programme. This allows you to see how successful the weight loss programme is, and also to ensure that your cat is not losing weight too quickly. It is also an opportunity to discuss any problems you might be having. Some

such problems we have discussed in **Section 2** including difficulties in increasing activity, feeding more than one cat and what to do if your cat is not losing weight. In addition at these check-up appointments be sure to mention any other problems that have arisen. Discussions may include:

■ Problems with the diet itself – is your cat eating the diet? Are they still hungry and asking for food after a meal?

■ Confession time – have you given extra treats/meals when your cat seemed hungry? Please don't be embarrassed to admit this, we all have done it! The veterinary staff need to know as this may mean a change of diet or feeding is required to avoid temptation in future

■ Update on activity levels – how are you finding playing with your cat? Would you like further advice on strategies to increase activity?

■ Any health concerns that have arisen – don't hesitate to mention them as soon as possible

■ Your frustrations – it may feel that you are working hard, spending money on special food and your cat is not losing weight, don't give up, chat to your veterinary staff and they can review your cat's case and help you find further motivation

What happens when my cat reaches target weight?

Hopefully after all of your efforts your cat has returned to a normal body condition score. Now is the time to consider how to maintain this weight. Do not lose touch with your veterinary practice as this can be a dangerous time when everyone relaxes, and your cat can easily gain back the weight and undo your hard work. It may be that now a diet change from a lower calorie food is required as further weight loss is not needed. However, this must be done carefully by working out how much of any new diet is needed to maintain your cat's weight, i.e. no further loss but certainly no gain. Your veterinary practice can advise you and you may feel happier sticking to a 'maintenance' or 'light' diet designed for such a situation. Do not relax on treats as this will add extra calories to the diet and can result in weight gain. Continue to increase your cat's activity as this fitness is beneficial at any weight and also adds to your cat's quality of life. It is worth continuing to have your cat weighed intermittently to ensure that the weight is not creeping on again.

During a cat's life, different stages may pose risks for weight gain, for example:

■ As cats get older their activity will reduce

■ Neutering can result in weight gain if the diet is not adjusted

■ If a cat used to going outdoors needs to be kept indoors for any reason, this may result in weight gain due to reduced activity

Therefore it is important to speak to your veterinary practice about feeding during different life stages.

If you own an overweight cat you are not alone! Please ask your veterinary practice for help as that is what they are there for, and when you are tempted to give up consider the following motivational tips:

Motivational tips for owners of overweight cats!

When you feel you are being cruel by restricting your cat's food intake and saying no to favourite treats, remember you are doing it for your cat's health and wellbeing and they will feel better and live longer if they can lose some weight

Weight loss in cats should, and usually does, take time. Rapid weight loss is dangerous so expect a slow and steady drop in numbers on the scales and plan for the weight loss to take months

Even 5 minutes of playing helps! When you are tired at the end of the day and just want to sit down in front of the TV, pick up a toy and spend just 5 minutes dangling it in front of your cat, every bit of activity helps

A new diet may cost more, and the trips to the vet initially may involve paying consultation fees, but if your cat develops health problems due to being overweight this can be much more expensive so by dealing with the problem now you can save healthcare costs in future

No diet goes completely smoothly. Yes there may be a day when you give in and let your cat lick the cream cheese tub! Don't give up on the whole diet because of this; it will still work if the occasional day doesn't go to plan

Be honest with yourself and your vet/nurse. If your cat isn't losing the weight as planned admit any extras you (or maybe a family member) have given, we are all human and will understand and can advise on some healthier treats

Get everyone 'on side'. Make sure the whole family understands the importance of the diet and sticks to it. What one person sees as a harmless treat can sabotage the entire weight loss regime if given frequently

In this section we have a look at some case examples of overweight cats and their treatment. They have been chosen to illustrate the problems that can be faced when dealing with an overweight cat.

'Boo' – the fat cat and the thin cat in the same house, how do we diet the right cat?

Boo's story illustrates the problems of putting one cat in a household on a diet whilst feeding the others normally.

Boo is a 6 year old, female neutered Siamese cross. She doesn't look very Siamese but certainly has a Siamese voice (loud and persistent!). She lives with 2 other cats, one is a lover of the outdoors, catcher of birds and generally very athletic. The other is an older cat who generally stays indoors and enjoys his retirement. Boo has access outdoors but prefers the company of humans indoors (and the sofa). Her carers are busy professionals and so don't have a lot of time at home.

The problem

Boo has always been a very greedy cat. As a kitten she lived with many other cats and perhaps had to compete for food. As a result she will eat anything and everything, including human food and the other cats' food if possible. She was neutered as a kitten and over the years has slowly gained weight. Each year she has been a little heavier and now is significantly overweight. She currently weighs 7kg and has a body condition score of 7/9 (4/5). Twice a day her carers fill up a bowl with dry, commercial adult cat food and also put out a sachet of wet food. The cats graze

Case example: 'Boo'

- Boo weighs 7kg and her ideal body weight is estimated to be 5.0kg

- 1% weight loss per week equals 70g

- The first goal weight after 1 month would therefore be 6.7kg

- It will take approximately 7 months for Boo to reach her ideal weight

- Using the equation mentioned in Section 2 Boo needs (30 x 5.0) + 70 = 220kcal per day

- 70% of this equals 154 kcal per day

- Her chosen diet contains 3500kcal per kg so Boo needs to eat 44g per day in order to lose weight

whilst their carers are at work. Boo's carers have noticed that she pounces on the food as soon as it is put down and they are not sure how much each cat is eating whilst they are out. In the evening they try and put food in front of the other cats but Boo continually tries to steal their food.

The dilemma

Boo certainly needs to go onto a calorie controlled diet. However, the other cats in the house are not overweight so do not need any calorie restriction, in fact the very active cat, and the older cat need more calories than Boo. Boo's carers do not play with her at the moment as they work long hours and come home tired. Boo is happy to sit around on the sofa all the time so doesn't exercise herself.

The treatment

Firstly Boo needs a check up at the veterinary practice to check she doesn't have any health problems either independent of or associated with her weight. On examination Boo was found to be in good health (apart from her weight), and blood tests did not show any problems.

Boo needs a daily measured portion of food containing the appropriate amount of calories, whilst the other cats need to be fed a normal diet. Currently Boo's owners have no idea how much she is eating and therefore how many calories she consumes each day. Therefore the following plan was established:

- Boo was used to, and preferred to eat dry food so a dry diet specially formulated to achieve weight loss was chosen

- Boo would be fed a measured amount of this diet and her weight loss supervised by her veterinary practice with a target weight loss of 1% per week (around 280g per month)

- Her carers decided that all of the cats should be fed 'portions' rather than an 'ad lib' feeding system so the other cats would be fed twice a day with standard commercial adult cat food. All of the cats would be fed earlier in the morning, with Boo fed separately in the bathroom, to allow longer for the slimmer cats to eat. The older cat who didn't go out would be shut in the lounge with a litter tray and an extra portion of food during the day

- In the evening the cats would again be fed their evening 'portion' but the athletic cat would be shut into the kitchen away from the other cats and fed an extra meal of his favourite wet food

- A few biscuits from Boo's allowance were put into a 'treat ball' for her to play with and eat during the day

- Her carers would designate 5-10 minutes a day to play with Boo with a fishing rod toy, every night, whilst watching the news on television!

- Boo would return to the practice every month to be weighed and to monitor her progress

The outcome

Initially Boo's carers found it difficult to separate the cats,

Boo looked a lot slimmer after her diet, and became more active.

prepare an extra meal for the older cat and stop Boo eating everyone else's food. Initially the slimmer cats, unused to portion feeding, did not finish their morning meal. However, they soon became accustomed to the change in their feeding regime and ate more at meal times. The extra feeds ensured that their weights remained stable, as planned. Boo was satisfied with her new food and didn't beg for treats as she finished her set meals and had playtime with her carers which she loved (as did the older cat, whose arthritis benefited from a little activity!). Boo's weight slowly dropped, and her carers sometimes felt frustrated that she lost small amounts at some checks, but they stuck with the plan and after 6 months she had lost 1 kg. This was a little less than the target but they continued with the diet and after another 3 months her weight was 5.5kg. At this point, Boo was reported to be much more active and her carers noticed that she was going outside more often.

The moral of the story

It can be really hard to put one cat in a multi-cat household on a diet and it is easy to ignore the one getting fatter! However, with effort a compromise can be found even with the very busy lives we all lead.

'Alfie' – two sides to every weight loss story

Alfie's story is told from the point of view of his very caring owner and also his veterinarian, who got their wires a little crossed initially, illustrating how communication and honesty between veterinary professionals and care providers is important.

Alfie is a lovely 12 year old male neutered black and white cat. He has enjoyed a stress-free life as the only pet of a cat-loving single lady. She is now retired and feels she and Alfie can enjoy retirement together. He has access to the outdoors but really would rather watch daytime TV on the sofa than move about too much.

The problem

Alfie is overweight and rather inactive. He really seems reluctant to move about much and avoids jumping where possible (apart from the occasion when the scones left on the kitchen table were too tempting…). He hates climbing stairs and does so very slowly. He is currently overweight at 6.9kg with a body condition score of 4/5 (7/9). He has a delicious diet of cooked chicken and fish, supplemented with tinned cat food of the most expensive kind. His carer describes him as fussy – as he really will not touch the cheaper brands and refuses the food the veterinarian gave her last time, a dry food for fat cats that is collecting dust in the cupboard. What follows is a story of two sides – both with the best intentions for Alfie – that illustrates some of the problems in managing overweight cats.

The care provider's story

Alfie's carer knows he is a little heavy, but feels very nervous taking him to the veterinary practice as she knows they will say he is overweight and insist on a strict diet that Alfie won't enjoy. She feels he is enjoying his retirement, is a little lazy, but generally happy. Why should she change things at this stage of his life? Alfie's carer gets a lot of pleasure from feeding him, cooking the fish just as he likes it and carefully selecting tins of tasty food she knows he will like. She is a little heavy herself and the doctor mentions it too but the nagging of doctors and veterinarians annoys her as she and Alfie like their treats and see nothing wrong in that. Alfie's carer loves Alfie very much and worries the veterinary staff will imply she is not a good care provider. However, Alfie is due his vaccination so a visit to the veterinarian is unavoidable but it is with trepidation that an appointment is made.

The veterinarian's story

The veterinarian, a recent graduate, is full of enthusiasm for every case she sees. She had lectures on overweight animals and knows the health problems that result from being overweight. She feels strongly that all overweight pets should be put on a diet and doesn't see any problems with this. She loves cats and was looking forward to her consultation with Alfie.

The consultation

As predicted on seeing Alfie our keen veterinarian starts to talk about his weight after checking him over and finding him well in all other ways. Alfie's carer immediately feels criticized and defensive, but tries to understand and purchases the relevant diet for fat cats from the receptionist on the way out. An appointment is booked for 3 weeks' time to assess Alfie's progress.

The bad outcome

Alfie's carer arrives home and opens the new bag of food. Alfie doesn't normally eat dry food so she is a little worried and not surprised when he refuses the food. However, she holds firm until about 10pm that evening when Alfie's pitiful mewing has the desired effect and a tin of sardines is opened. Alfie goes to bed happy whilst his care provider is frustrated and a little less confident in her veterinarian's advice. The next day she cancels the check-up appointment.

What went wrong?

Earlier in the book we discussed the importance of diet but also the importance of exercise. Alfie was perceived as lazy, and perhaps he was, but his veterinarian should maybe have listened a little harder to his carer when she mentioned he didn't move about much. Alfie is of an age when osteoarthritis can develop. In cats this often causes a reduction in mobility and reluctance to climb stairs. Alfie has painful joints and so lies on the sofa all day. Also Alfie's carer dotes on him and derives a lot of pleasure from feeding him. She needs a diet plan that firstly includes a diet he likes and secondly allows for some healthy treats. She also needs support. A cat like Alfie may be set in his ways and so his care provider needs guidance and more advice than can be given in a short consultation. Alfie also may need some treatment for his joint pain to allow him to move about more.

The solution

Alfie's veterinarian had been looking forward to seeing him again and was disappointed when the appointment was cancelled. She had a feeling Alfie's carer was worried by what she said and after discussing the case with one of the nurses she decided to call Alfie's carer. She asked her if she would come to a weight management clinic appointment with the nurse who had recently started running such clinics. She was sorry to hear Alfie didn't like his food and promised to talk to the nurse about some alternatives. Alfie's carer reluctantly attended the clinic and found the nurse very sympathetic. She told her all about how Alfie doesn't move about much and likes his favourite foods. A compromise was found by firstly writing down everything Alfie ate and trying Alfie on a wet diet food that was more similar to his usual diet, and introducing it slowly, mixing his favourite fish with the food to make the taste more familiar. Particularly high calorie treats were cut out of the diet. The calories in his cooked fish and chicken were calculated and a diet plan that included such foods was formulated. After checking Alfie's liver and kidney function with a blood and urine test his veterinarian also prescribed a pain killer to help his osteoarthritis.

The good outcome

Alfie's carer felt a lot better after this visit to the veterinary practice and made sure she kept the regular nurse weight clinic appointments. She couldn't believe how Alfie had started to move up and down stairs with ease and would even casually bat a piece of string dangled over him. He wasn't mad on his new food but would accept it as long as he was allowed a little of what he liked. He slowly lost weight over the next 12 months and both care provider and cat enjoyed their retirement all the more.

The moral of the story

When changing routines the relationship between the care provider and the cat must be considered and realistic goals set. Continued support is vital, for example, via nurses' clinics. When dealing with older cats, conditions resulting in pain and reluctance to move must be taken into account and treated if possible.

Each cat and each care provider are different so weight loss programmes must be tailored to each different situation for them to be successful.

'Lulu' – the guilt and the diabetes

This case shows the diseases that can result from obesity and how hard work from dedicated carers can turn the situation around.

Lulu is an 8 year old female neutered Domestic-shorthaired cat and her story is told completely by her care providers as it is inspiring but, as her carers admit, it was a rocky road to get where they are now. *Text in italics has been added by Sam and Andrea to explain the veterinary side of things.*

'We picked up Lulu as a 12 week old kitten from our local rescue centre. We had lost our old cat at 18 years old just a few months before and the house felt empty without a cat in it. She was a small bundle of fur when we took her home but quickly settled in. We took her to be neutered at 6 months old as we had been advised by our veterinarian. She had been fed on a dry food diet at the rescue centre and we continued to feed her this diet, with treats and tuna fish (her favorite) during her life, choosing the type designed for adult cats once she was old enough.

We really didn't notice she had put weight on until she was about 3 or 4 years old when friends would joke she looked pregnant! She had that bit of fat hanging down under her belly that cats get. At yearly vaccinations the veterinarian would mention Lulu's weight and we would cut down the treats a little

but she slowly got bigger. It was such a slow increase we didn't worry and she was rather lazy, spending her days on the sofa!

When Lulu was 8 years old she started to drink more water. We noticed she was drinking out of the pond outside (which was unusual for her) and took her to the veterinary practice. They were a little alarmed at her size and I certainly felt embarrassed when she tipped the scales at nearly 7.5kg or nearly 17lbs. The veterinarian took a blood test and phoned us later in the day with the results. He said her blood sugar was too high and he needed to run another test at the lab (*fructosamine, a measure of blood sugars over a week or so to confirm* diabetes) to see if she was diabetic. This came as a total shock to us as we had assumed she had a water infection or something else easy to treat. We waited a horrible few days to find out the result from the laboratory. It confirmed her diabetes and we were told to come back to the veterinary practice for a chat about insulin. I have an uncle who is diabetic and remember seeing him give himself injections and I was horrified at Lulu having to have jabs. I am not a fan of needles and my husband works long hours so couldn't help and I was terrified of doing everything wrong. At the veterinary practice I had a long consultation with our veterinarian who explained that the diabetes might be due to Lulu being so heavy and that we needed to change her diet as well as start injections, which he showed me how to do. He also checked her blood pressure and took a urine sample (*to check for infections that can make* diabetes *harder to control*). To be honest this was a lot to take in, as was the large bill when I left. My husband and I felt so guilty that we had caused Lulu to have to go through all of this discomfort – if only we had done something about her weight sooner.

> **"we really didn't notice she had put weight on until friends joked she looked pregnant!"**

We were sent home with a bag of needles, insulin and a bag and tins of a new food (*a high* protein, *low* carbohydrate *diet, shown in studies to be very useful in contributing to reversal of* diabetes *in some cases*). We were given an appointment to go back in one week for another blood test to see how the treatment was going. Actually the injecting was ok and Lulu seemed unconcerned. She wasn't mad on the new food mind you and we mixed a bit of her favorite tuna into it to encourage her to eat it as the veterinarian had explained it was important she kept eating to avoid low blood sugars (*and* hepatic lipidosis).

We went back to the veterinary practice after a week and for several other appointments that month. The veterinarian said Lulu was doing well and had lost some weight already. The bills were alarming but what could we do? We love Lulu and wanted her to get better. We joined the practice's weight management nurses group and I felt it was easier to talk to the nurse as she had more time than the veterinarian. Things were going better until one day when Lulu refused her food. We didn't know what to do so we offered her some of her old food and she ate keenly. In hindsight we should have contacted the veterinarian as after this she refused to eat the new diet and at our next visit she had gained weight. I felt embarrassed to admit she had been eating the 'wrong' food but the nurse understood and we basically started again with the diabetic diet by mixing a little of the old food into the new food and slowly reducing the amount of the old food. The nurse also advised playing with Lulu to increase her activity. I was very skeptical as she is such a lazy cat but even her leisurely batting a fishing toy was better than nothing the nurse explained (*we agree, any activity helps and also makes a cat's life more interesting*). After another few weeks Lulu returned to the veterinary hospital for a blood test and a great improvement in her blood sugar was seen, so much that her insulin dose was lowered. She was now down to 7.2kg and moving about more at home. This improvement spurred us on and we really stuck to the diet now (before I admit to the odd lick of butter from my toast!). After another month she was down to 6.9kg and the veterinarian asked us to stop the insulin. We were worried that this wasn't right but he explained that by using the diet and achieving the weight loss, her diabetes was so controlled that she no longer needed insulin injections (*yes, some diabetic cats can stop requiring insulin injections if they lose weight and eat the right diet. Of course if you have a diabetic cat, never stop insulin unless your veterinarian tells you to*).

Lulu is now 6.5kg after 6 months of treatment and her blood sugar is normal. We have spent an awful amount of money and wish we had tackled her weight before she became diabetic as it would have saved money and all those injections, and our guilt at having caused our lovely cat all this trouble. I would advise anyone to look at their cat with fresh eyes and speak to the veterinarian about their weight. Also I would advise going to a nurse's clinic as the encouragement they gave us really helped and I found the nurses very easy to talk to.

'Thomas' – an example of how quickly weight gain can occur when food intake is not regulated

Thomas is an 11 year old MN DSH cat, who lives with one other cat, Jack. They have a predominantly indoor lifestyle, with intermittent outdoor access at their request when the owner is at home, although they never choose to stay outside for long! Neither of them are hunters. They are both fed together, 80% wet commercial cat food, and 20% dry food given in a food ball and puzzle feeders.

The owner went on holiday for 4 weeks and a friend moved into the house to look after the cats. Their environment and lifestyle therefore didn't change. Feeding instructions were left – 1 sachet of wet food for each cat twice daily, and a tiny handful of dry food to be left in the puzzle feeder.

The cats before the owner went on holiday.

Picture 1 below shows Thomas when the owner arrived back from holiday! No additional treats had been offered and the same amount of wet food had been fed. Unfortunately, the friend's interpretation of a tiny handful of dry food was much more than the owner's interpretation! This serves to emphasise how weight gain can so easily occur with what appears to be no change in food intake. It also illustrates how difficult it is for owners to accurately measure and limit the amount of dry food offered and how important this is in maintaining a healthy bodyweight.

Picture 2 below shows Thomas 12 weeks after starting a weight loss programme, illustrating that successful weight loss can be achieved in cats when food intake is strictly regulated.

SECTION 5 | further information

There are many carers with overweight cats and the support of others can be very useful when your cat is on a diet or you are worried about your cat's weight. Sources of support in the form of chat rooms and online forums are available via the internet. Remember that many sites haven't been checked by a veterinarian and that advice may be the personal opinion of the individual offering it, and they do not always know your cat and your situation. Always check with your veterinarian before changing your cat's diet.

The following sites will provide general information on cat care:
Feline Advisory Bureau: www.fabcats.org
The Blue Cross: www.bluecross.org.uk
Cat's Protection: www.cats.org.uk
American Association of Feline Practitioners: www.catvets.com
The Royal Society for the Prevention of Cruelty to Animals: www.rspca.org.uk

Specific information on managing overweight cats:
www.fabcats.org/owners/feeding/overweight.html
www.hillspet.co.uk
www.royalcanin.co.uk
www.iams.co.uk
www.purina.co.uk

Information on care of indoor cats:
Indoor cat initiative: http://indoorpet.osu.edu/index.cfm

Information on fencing gardens and making cat enclosures:
www.cdpets.com
www.purrfectfence.com
www.fabcats.org/owners/fencing/info.html
www.fabcats.org/owners/fencing/info2.html

Information on cat behaviour:
Vicky Halls: www.vickyhalls.net – Vicky is an internationally recognised expert in feline behaviour

Information on cystitis
'Caring for a cat with lower urinary tract disease' published by Cat Professional, www.catprofessional.com

Glossary of terms used by veterinarians

Term	Definition
Ad libitum/'ad lib'	In reference to feeding this phrase means offering a constant, usually unlimited, supply of food that the cat can eat as they please during the day/night.
Amino acids	Small individual molecules that that get joined up to make the proteins found in the diet. Cats have a requirement for certain amino acids that they must find in their food or they may develop health problems.
Anaesthetic/anaesthesia	Providing a state of unconsciousness, muscle relaxation and loss of pain sensation using certain drugs (usually a combination of intravenous administration and by gas inhalation).
Arthritis	See ostoeoarthritis.
Body condition score (BCS)	A way of measuring a cat's body condition that is independent of weight on the scales, as this can be misleading. For example, a domestic short hair cat weighing 8 kg might be considered to be overweight, whereas a Maine Coon weighing the same might be considered to be a healthy weight. Using a scale from underweight to overweight (usually 1-5 or 1-9) a cat is allocated a number according to how much fat they are carrying on their body.
Calorie/s	Units of energy found in food or drink (e.g. milk). Consumption of excess calories can result in weight gain.
Carbohydrates	Sugars and starches found in food which are broken down to provide energy. Cats are less able to use carbohydrates than other animals, relying more on proteins.
Carnivore	An animal (in this case cats), that feeds on other animals. Cats are 'obligate carnivores' meaning they must eat meat to get all the nutrients they need.
Complementary diet	A diet that if fed alone will not provide all of the nutrients a cat needs and may result in deficiencies and illness. Can be fed as part of a balanced diet with other foods. If the diet is a complementary diet it should be stated on the packaging.
Complete diet	A diet containing all the nutrients a cat needs. No additional food will be required when feeding this type of diet. If the diet is a complete diet it should be stated on the packaging.
Constipation	Infrequent passage of often hard, dry stools. Obesity can cause or worsen constipation as affected cats may move around less. Treatment in addition to a change of diet includes laxatives available from your veterinarian and ensuring adequate water intake.

Term	Definition
Cystitis	Inflammation of the urinary bladder (where urine is stored before urination), a painful condition. Signs of cystitis include blood in the urine, straining to urinate and producing small amounts or no urine. Although this can be caused by a range of problems including bacterial infections, bladder stones and tumours, the most common cause is 'feline idiopathic cystitis' (FIC). FIC can be triggered or exacerbated by stress and obese cats are more vulnerable to this condition.
Dehydration	A serious condition in which an affected cat has lost more fluid than they have drunk. Fluid can be lost via vomiting/diarrhoea and also into the urine due to conditions such as diabetes or kidney problems. Signs include depression, sunken eyes, dry mouth and loss of skin elasticity. The condition requires immediate veterinary treatment.
Diabetes (diabetes mellitus)	This condition is seen in middle-aged to older cats and results from a lack of insulin, or an inability of the body to respond to insulin, a hormone produced by the pancreas that allows the body to use sugars to make energy. Signs include weight loss, drinking and urinating excessively and in severe cases vomiting, diarrhoea and lethargy. It is diagnosed via blood +/- urine tests and treatment involves diet, insulin injections and a weight loss programme, if needed. Obese cats are more likely to suffer from diabetes.
Fat (fatty acids)	An energy source found in food and stored in the body (to excess in overweight cats). Cats have a requirement for some small fats (fatty acids) that they must find in their diets (called essential fatty acids). Excessive energy consumed will be stored in the body as fat.
Feline idiopathic cystitis	A form of cystitis, common in cats, where there is no bacterial infection and causes are thought to include stress. Obesity can also contribute to the development of this painful condition.
Fibre	Fibrous material from fruits and vegetables used to 'bulk' up some weight loss diets.
Geriatric	Term used to describe older cats. The definition varies but usually describes cats over 12 years of age.
Hepatic lipidosis	A serious and often fatal condition of the liver which can be the result of an overweight cat losing weight too quickly.

Term	Definition
Insulin	A hormone that allows the body to use sugars for energy – see diabetes mellitus.
Kibble	Another term for a piece of dry food (also may be referred to as a biscuit).
L-carnitine	An amino acid derivative often found in weight loss diets that increases the break-down of fat and helps retain muscle mass.
Lower urinary tract disease	Also see cystitis. A spectrum of problems affecting a cat's urinary tract resulting in cystitis and in some cases obstruction of the urethra (tube through which urine passes from the bladder to the outside) resulting in an inability to urinate. A painful and serious condition that obese cats appear to be more prone to.
Metabolism	Chemical processes taking place in the body to break down food to create energy and keep the body healthy.
Neutering	In male cats the removal of the testicles and in females the removal of the ovaries and usually also the uterus (ovariohysterectomy, removal of the female reproductive organs). Commonly called 'spaying' for female cats.
Obese/obesity	A condition where affected cats are at least 15-20% heavier than their ideal body weight.
Overweight	A cat is described as overweight if they are above their ideal weight, usually 10-19% over.
Omnivore	An animal that eats meat and vegetables for example humans or dogs.
Osteoarthritis/arthritis	Inflammation of the joints. Typically seen in older cats and results in pain moving around. Affected cats often have trouble jumping up, climbing stairs and may be less active than normal. Treatment in the form of painkillers is available, under prescription, from the veterinary practice. Being overweight may make arthritis worse and affected cats will benefit from weight loss.

Term	Definition
Protein	The building blocks of body tissues and an essential part of a cat's diet as cats use protein as an energy source.
Prescription diet	A specially formulated diet designed for a specific health condition such as feline obesity. Usually only available from your veterinary practice and should only be fed with veterinary advice and supervision.
Systemic hypertension	High blood pressure. Seen in older cats and may result in serious consequences, therefore it is important for older cats to have their blood pressure checked.